# Victory in Jesus

### Bible Object Lessons about Jesus for Kids

ANNE MARIE GOSNELL

**Victory in Jesus: Bible Object Lessons About Jesus for Kids**

© 2019 Anne Marie Gosnell. All rights reserved. Permission is given to use said document in a home, school, church, or co-op setting. This document may not be transmitted in any other form or by any other means—electronic, mechanical, photocopying, recording, or otherwise—without prior written permission of Anne Marie Gosnell. Coloring pages may be copied for classroom lessons.

ISBN: 978-0-9981968-7-9 (print), 978-0-9981968-8-6 (epub)

Scripture quotations taken from the New American Standard Bible® (NASB), Copyright © 1960, 1962, 1963, 1968, 1971, 1972, 1973, 1975, 1977, 1995 by The Lockman Foundation. Used by permission. www.Lockman.org

ICB — Scripture taken from the International Children's Bible®. Copyright © 1986, 1988, 1999 by Thomas Nelson. Used by permission. All rights reserved.

Publishing and Design Services: MartinPublishingServices.com

"Jesus was the master of using object lessons and the Gospels are full of them. I believe they are the best way to visually teach people of every age especially children! I love this book because it's so easy to use and it's full of practical truths. Thanks, Anne Marie, for all you do to help kids and teachers soar!"

—**JIM WIDEMAN**, Kidmin Pioneer, https://jimwideman.com

"Looking for object lessons that you can use when you teach children from the Gospels? Each lesson in the Victory of Jesus study gives you a supply list, a section of scripture to learn and prepare to paraphrase for your students, background information, and questions to discuss with your students. The object lesson helps to get the children focused for the lesson and reinforces the lesson application. Great for teachers of children!"

—**DIANNA WIEBE**, Author and Bible teacher

"My friend and fellow author has done it again! Anne Marie Gosnell, who has been producing family and church ministry resources for years, has released a new object lesson book, all about the gospels! Lessons include the nativity, the child Jesus, a bit of geography and history from Jesus time and so much more! This is a great tool that even comes with free posters. Excellent for Sunday school, kid's church, VBS, camps, Christmas and Easter events and family devotions! An excellent choice for pastors, teachers and parents alike!!"

—**TRISH PEACH**, author of *Your Children's Ministry From Scratch*, *Your Children's Ministry Beyond Basics*, and *Why We Quit*, www.kidmin.ninja

"Anne Marie has put together a resource that is easily used and understood by the novice Bible teacher or the experienced leader. This is a source of encouragement with the goal of transforming anyone into a person equipped for the work of teaching. All you need is a willingness to learn and grow!"

—**JOE M. BRIDGER, MACFM**, Children's Pastor, Spring Arbor Free Methodist Church, Spring Arbor Michigan

# DEDICATION

■ ■ ■ ■ ■ ■ ■ ■ ■ ■ ■ ■ ■ ■ ■ ■ ■ ■ ■ ■ ■

To Roy, Faith, and Leah.

I love watching you grow in your faith!

# CONTENTS

Dedication ........................................................................... v

Introduction ........................................................................ 1

How This Book Works ....................................................... 2

A Few Last Tips .................................................................. 4

The Annunciation ............................................................... 5

The Nativity ....................................................................... 12

Jesus as a Child ................................................................ 18

John the Baptist ............................................................... 23

Jesus in the Wilderness .................................................. 30

Jesus Calls the Twelve Disciples .................................... 36

Jesus' First Miracles ........................................................ 42

Jesus and Nicodemus ..................................................... 48

The Woman at the Well ................................................... 55

Jesus Heals the Lame Man ............................................. 61

# CONTENTS

Feeding the Five Thousand ..................................................................................... 67

The Beatitudes ........................................................................................................ 73

Jesus Heals the Blind Man ..................................................................................... 80

The Kingdom of Heaven ......................................................................................... 87

Jesus is the Good Shepherd .................................................................................. 95

The Passover ........................................................................................................ 101

The Passion of Jesus ............................................................................................ 109

The Resurrection .................................................................................................. 115

The Road to Emmaus ........................................................................................... 120

Bread and Fish by the Sea ................................................................................... 127

Make Disciples of the Nations .............................................................................. 134

How to Lead a Child to Christ ............................................................................... 143

How to Become an Excellent Bible Teacher ........................................................ 146

A Note from the Author ......................................................................................... 149

Coloring Pages ..................................................................................................... 151

# INTRODUCTION

■■■■■■■■■■■■■■■■■■■■■

*Victory in Jesus: Bible Object Lessons About Jesus for Kids* includes 21 interactive object lessons for children ages 5 to 12. These weekly lessons are meant to last 20-30 minutes. I believe the title, *Victory in Jesus*, correctly depicts God's idea of salvation. Before we recognized that we were sinners, God planned for Jesus to die a sacrificial death in our place. This gives us victory!

This curriculum will help you:

- teach engaging Bible lessons children cannot resist;
- create a fun teaching atmosphere that sparks the imagination of children;
- teach children Biblical truth that enhances their spiritual growth; and
- share the gospel with children and expand the Kingdom.

I am humbled that you have chosen to use this resource! I pray that it will ignite a passion for Jesus in those who hear you teach.

**For the extra resources for this book, visit**
https://www.futureflyingsaucers.com/vij

**FREE Gift!** Please visit
https://youtu.be/-80GiTQpbQI
to watch the first session of the course Becoming an Excellent Bible Teacher.

**To receive weekly Bible lessons, book updates, and children's ministry helps, subscribe at**
https://www.futureflyingsaucers.com

Keep on keeping on, my friend!

Anne Marie Gosnell
futureflyingsaucers.com

# HOW THIS BOOK WORKS

I have put these lessons in an order that encourages spiritual growth. However, the lessons do not have to be taught sequentially. These lessons can be taught with large groups or small groups. When planning your Bible lessons, whether at home or church, determine your objective first. Then look through the Table of Contents and decide which lessons will best help you reach your objective.

Each lesson has a **free downloadable poster** that you can access from the **Resources Page** (https://www.futureflyingsaucers.com/vij). Discuss and display the posters in the room throughout this series, and read them each week. You can choose to use the shorter verses as memory verses. Other lesson freebies can also be found on the Resources Page (https://www.futureflyingsaucers.com/vij).

Many lessons have a **Background** section. This summarizes the events that "set the stage" for the lesson. Use this section to help you put the lesson into context for the children.

New Testament history takes place in a variety of locations; therefore, there is a **Geography** section for each lesson. I encourage you to have a map to point out these places. See the Resources Page (https://www.futureflyingsaucers.com/vij) for maps.

The **Object Lesson** is usually first and might be referred to throughout the lesson. Most of the objects are items that many children know and see daily. Jesus used common objects such as sheep and trees when He taught, and we can do the same. Preparation time is minimal, and most lessons use materials you will find around your home. I do suggest practicing the lessons ahead of time to be sure you understand how the activity works.

The **Bible Lesson** section is a paraphrase of the event from the **Scripture Focus**. Read the Scripture to prepare for teaching your lesson. Afterward, read the Bible Lesson section a few times. Practice enough that you can tell the story without reading.

The last section is essential: **Life Application**. This is where Scripture "comes alive" and the kids learn how to apply it to their lives. If we do not explain the

## HOW THIS BOOK WORKS

purpose of Scripture to children, then you and I have failed as Bible teachers. All Scripture is useful, and we must showcase the glorious purpose of the Bible in each lesson.

At the end of each lesson is a **Comment Box**. This is an area for you to reflect upon your teaching so you can improve your skills. Thinking retrospectively will help you to evaluate your personal ministry. Ask yourself two questions: *"What went well as I taught this lesson?"* and *"What can I do better?"*

For more in-depth Bible teacher training, take a look at my online course, "Becomng an Excellent Bible Teacher" (https://futureflyingsaucers-bible-institute.teachable.com/p/excellent-bible-teacher).

I would love to know how your lessons go! Feel free to contact me at futureflyingsaucers@klopex.com. You can also join my Facebook group, Become an Excellent Bible Teacher: Bible Lessons for Kids (https://www.facebook.com/groups/BibleLessonsForKids).

To tell me what you think about this book, please visit Amazon.com and leave me an honest review. It will be greatly appreciated.

*But thanks be to God, who gives us the victory through our Lord Jesus Christ!*

—*1 Corinthians 15:57*

# A FEW LAST TIPS

Encourage the children to use their Bibles. Do not assume they think your story is Biblical just because you tell it. Have them be like the Bereans in the book of Acts. Show them in the Bible the verses you will be using. Some of the lessons will have the kids either reading along with you or reading for themselves. If you have children who do not read, you can still help them find the reference in the Bible. This is a great habit to begin when young.

When you teach a lesson, try not to say words such as, *"Our story today comes from..."* While the Bible is the story of God, it is more than a story. We live in a world where the line between fairy tales, fiction, and truth is blurred. Because of this, refer to every person or event as history or biography. Children need to understand that people in Scripture were **real**, breathing people. The places in the Bible were—and some still are—**real** places.

Be enthusiastic when you teach. Do not put on a show, but share the joy of Jesus so that He is contagious! Scripture tells us that if Jesus is lifted up, He will draw all men to Him. Let us lift Him up!

One last thing...NEVER be afraid to share your testimony! Someone in the room might need to hear how God has worked in your past, how He is working today, and what He is doing in your future.

# 1 THE ANNUNCIATION

∎∎∎∎∎∎∎∎∎∎∎∎∎∎∎∎∎∎∎∎

Splitting the Red Sea and walking on dry land...city walls falling down...chariots of fire? The Bible is filled with events that sound impossible. In this lesson, talk about the conversations Gabriel had with Zachariah (or Zacharias) and Mary, and how God continues to do the impossible.

**Scripture Focus:** Luke 1:5-40

**Materials:**

- Joke book (or funny stories that will make the children laugh)
- Poster for Luke 1:37

**Geography:** Galilee, Nazareth

**Background:** God had been silent, but still working, for 400 years.

THE ANNUNCIATION

# OBJECT LESSON

**{Pull out the jokes or funny stories. Ask:}**

Do you like to laugh? Do you like to tell jokes? [*Allow answers*]

**{Read three or four jokes and enjoy them with the children.}**

God created us to smile and laugh. He enjoys us and likes to bless us. While I think God has a great sense of humor, I do not think God jokes around. If you think about it, jokes are meant to trick someone or to make fun of something. God does not do that. He never tricks us. He is always honest with us. That was what Zachariah and Mary found out.

THE ANNUNCIATION

# BIBLE LESSON

**{Read Luke 1:5-40.}**

It was Zachariah's turn to go to the temple. His lot had been cast. This meant Zachariah's name was drawn from the group of available priests. He went to Jerusalem to serve for two weeks.

Zachariah was an old man, and his wife was old as well. He was a priest and had no children to whom to pass on the priesthood. He was righteous and blameless, and he walked in the commands of God.

It was Zachariah's turn to go into the temple and burn the incense. This offering was given twice a day. The people were standing outside the temple as Zachariah went in. Those who had gathered were praying because the incense that Zachariah was offering symbolized the prayers of the nation of Israel.

**{Ask:}**

- How do you think Zachariah felt when he saw an angel? [*Allow for answers; remind them God had been silent for 400 years. Zachariah was troubled, or scared.*]

- What were the first words the angel said? [*"Do not be afraid."*]

- What other couple have you learned about who had a baby in their old age? [*Abraham and Sarah*]

- What prayer do you think was heard? [*Allow for answers. The priest was to go in and offer the incense which represented all of the prayers of Israel. This was a serious job. It is also possible that Zachariah had been praying for a son, or even for the coming of the Messiah.*]

- What message did the angel give to Zachariah? [*His wife Elizabeth was going to have a baby, and the baby's name should be John.*]

- Why do you think God sent an angel to deliver this message? [*Allow for answers. This was the beginning of an amazing event…the Good News was coming! Such a message deserved a celestial messenger.*]

- How would Zachariah and others feel when John was born? [*They would feel joy and gladness, and many would rejoice.*]

# THE ANNUNCIATION

This event is called the Annunciation. The word *annunciation* means an announcement. Gabriel announced to Zachariah that his wife would have a son and that the baby would make the people ready for the Lord.

When he saw the angel, it was almost like Zachariah asked the angel if God was joking. However, God was about to start the events that would save His people from their sins. It was to begin with Zachariah, a righteous man whom God wanted to bless in his old age.

God was being serious. But God does not do things the way people think He should.

**{Ask:}**

- What was the consequence for Zachariah's unbelief? [*He was not allowed to speak until the prophecy came true. He was a priest and knew the prophesies; he had no excuse for his disbelief.*]
- How did all of the people respond when Zachariah finally came out of the temple? [*They had been waiting and thought it was strange that Zachariah had taken so long. When Zachariah came out and could not speak, they understood that he had seen a vision.*]
- What happened to Elizabeth? [*She became pregnant.*]
- After four months, what did Elizabeth do? Why? [*She hid herself. When women become pregnant, their bellies swell and the baby cannot be hidden.*]
- What was the name of the angel who told both announcements? [*Gabriel*]
- What were the first words told to Mary by the angel? [*"Rejoice! Highly favored one!"*]
- How must Mary have felt seeing this angel? [*She was probably scared, but the angel told her not to be afraid.*]
- How does one find favor with God? What pleases Him? [*Read Hebrews 11:6. Without faith it is impossible to please God. To find favor, we must believe that God exists and that He rewards those who diligently (actively) seek Him.*]
- What would Mary's baby be called? [*Jesus, the Son of the Highest*]
- What was Jesus going to be? [*A King*]

Elizabeth was old and was going to have a baby. This was strange! However, Elizabeth knew that God had not forgotten her. God had decided to finally bless her with a baby so people in the town would not disapprove of her anymore. In Jewish society, if a woman was barren (not able to have a baby), people disapproved, or thought the woman was sinful in God's sight.

Mary went to her cousin's house. Mary had a different problem than Elizabeth. She was going to have a baby. She was engaged to Joseph, but they were not married yet. Having a baby when you were not married was a scandal! It was considered a bad thing. Mary knew that the people around her would not be happy.

Perhaps Mary went to Elizabeth's house because she knew that Elizabeth was going through a strange time as well. Both ladies wanted to hide from people. Two very special ladies, who were going to have two very special babies, needed each other.

**{Ask:}**

- Is anything impossible with God? [*No*]
- List some other "impossible" things God has done throughout the Bible, and also in YOUR life. [*Allow for answers; possible answers include splitting the Red Sea, the sun standing still, wrestling with an angel, etc. Lead the children to think about Jesus raising Lazarus. Then introduce the idea of Jesus dying on the cross and then God raising Him from the dead.*]

# LIFE APPLICATION

■ ■ ■ ■ ■ ■ ■ ■ ■ ■ ■ ■ ■ ■ ■ ■ ■ ■ ■ ■

God enjoys His people, but He does not joke around with us. He takes Himself, us, and sin seriously. He is Truth. He will always tell you the truth. He will not hide from you. He wants you to seek Him. He wants to show you that He can do the impossible.

The Bible is filled with prophesies, such as a King being born in the town of Bethlehem... or one who would prepare the way before the Lord (Isaiah 40:3; Malachi 3:1).

Even though Zachariah had a lack of faith, Elizabeth and Mary were committed to God's will right from the start. They did not know how their lives would change, but they knew God would take care of them.

God takes care of you, too. Sometimes He does the impossible. Sometimes He asks US to do impossible things. But if you are committed to Him, even if your life changes, God will take care of you.

If you are committed to Jesus and repent of (turn away from) your sins, God will forgive you. How amazing it is that an all-powerful, righteous God would forgive the sins of rebellious people like us. It sounds impossible, but it is true.

**What can we learn from the Annunciation to Zachariah and Mary? No matter how impossible something sounds, if God tells you it will happen... then it will happen. He is trustworthy.**

# COMMENT BOX

**THINK:** What went well as you taught this lesson? What can you do better?

_____
_____
_____
_____
_____
_____
_____
_____
_____
_____

**TIP:** Try to bring Jesus and salvation into every lesson that you teach.

# 2 THE NATIVITY

Have you looked at your nativity scene lately? Have you ever thought if it matches up to what Scripture says? In this lesson, take a fun and in-depth look at what Scripture says happened the night Jesus was born.

**Scripture Focus:** Luke 2:1-20 and Mathew 2:1-12

**Materials:**

- Your baby picture
- Empty picture frame
- Nativity scene with shepherds, angels, animals, wise men, and family
- Poster of Luke 2:11

**Geography:** Galilee, Nazareth, Bethlehem

**Background:** The Law had been given. The Old Testament was over. The Romans were the most powerful empire in the world. Roads had been built, and most people spoke a common language. The time was perfect for a special baby to be born.

# OBJECT LESSON

**{Show the baby picture, but do not tell the children who it is. Have the children list different fun and not-so-fun things about having a newborn baby. Explain that you have another baby picture to show as well. Only show the back of the frame.}**

Adam and Eve were the first people to sin. When Adam and Eve had the first baby, that baby was born into sin. Every baby born since then has a sin problem, or a sin nature.

The baby shown in this next frame LOVES the baby who is in the first picture. In fact, this second baby was born to save the first baby.

**{Turn the empty frame around. Ask:}**

- Who is the baby that was born to save this first baby? [*Jesus*]
- Why is there no picture of Baby Jesus? [*There are no pictures of Baby Jesus that exist. In fact, there is no real likeness of Him at any stage of life.*]

We do not know what Jesus looked like, but we know that He was God in human flesh. **It is like God put on a costume.** God isn't human. Jesus, who is God, took off His glory, left it in Heaven, and put on the flesh of man. He chose to be human to fix our sin nature. You might choose a costume to wear and pretend to be something you really are not. But the neat thing about Jesus is that **His costume was real**. Jesus really was human. He was God AND He was human.

The first chapter of John tells us that Jesus was with God when He created the world. And then verse 14 tells us that Jesus became a man and lived on the earth.

THE NATIVITY

# BIBLE LESSON

There are many traditions that Christians talk about, act out, and assume during Christmas. And many times, the traditions ADD to Scripture, which can be dangerous. **We want to *know* what God's Word says, not *assume* we know what it says**. We do not want to add information that is not in Scripture.

**{Use the nativity scene to set up the events of Jesus' birth as you read them. Read Luke 2:1-20 and then Mathew 2:1-12. Ask:}**

- Was Jesus born the first night Mary and Joseph were in Bethlehem? [*No, He was born while they were there.*]

- Did Mary ride a donkey? [*Scripture does not say, but many people traveled by donkey during Biblical times.*]

- Was Jesus born in a stable? Or a cave? [*Scripture does not say, but there was a manger, and Jesus was laid in it.*]

- Did the inn keeper help Mary and Joseph? [*Scripture does not say. It only says that there was no room in the inn.*]

- Did the shepherds visit at day or night? [*The angels appeared at night, so the shepherds went to town after the angels left them.*]

- Was Jesus born during the day or night? [*Scripture does not say.*]

- Was Jesus born just outside of Bethlehem? [*No, He was born in town, because the angels said "in the city of David" and the shepherds went to town. In this region of Israel, people built their homes over caves. The caves would house the animals. So it is possible that Jesus was born in a cave, although scripture does not explicitly tell us that.*]

- Why was Jesus born in Bethlehem? [*Bethlehem is called "the city of David," which causes us to think about King David and the promise God gave him. God told David that He would establish his throne forever. Jesus was a decendant of King David and Jesus is the Eternal King. Bethlehem also fulfills a prophesy about the Messiah. 2 Samuel 7:13, Micah 5:2*]

- Did the multitude of angels sing? [*Scripture says they praised God and "said," not sang.*]

# THE NATIVITY

- How many people did the shepherds tell about Baby Jesus? [*The shepherds told many people about Baby Jesus because they made it widely known.*]

- Were the wise men there the same night as the shepherds? [*No, because Scripture says "after Jesus was born" and they "saw the child," not a baby.*]

- Did the wise men really "follow" a star? [*A star appeared in the sky. We are not told about it moving until it reappeared after the wise men saw Herod.*]

- How many wise men were there? [*Scripture does not say.*]

- Did the wise men ride on camels? [*Scripture does not say, but people in the East probably did ride camels.*]

- Who was troubled by the wise men? [*King Herod*]

- Where were Joseph, Mary, and Jesus living? [*In a house*]

- How old was Jesus? [*Scripture calls Jesus a child and not a baby, so He may have been two or three years old.*]

- How many gifts did the wise men give? [*Only three are listed.*]

- How do you think the nativity scene should be set up? [*Allow for answers.*]

- What would you do differently? [*Allow for answers.*]

- Would you add or take away characters? [*Allow for answers.*]

**{In my house, the wise men are traveling and placed away from Baby Jesus.}**

- Can you think of Christmas plays, shows, or songs that say something incorrect about the Christmas story? [*Allow for answers.*]

# LIFE APPLICATION

■ ■ ■ ■ ■ ■ ■ ■ ■ ■ ■ ■ ■ ■ ■ ■ ■ ■ ■ ■ ■ ■ ■

Many times, we think we know everything about a Bible event because it is familiar to us. Once we start to consistently read God's Word, we realize that there is much we never knew.

**Satan would LOVE for us to not know the story of Jesus.** However, God wants us to be *smart Christians*. He wants us to read His words and think about them. He wants us to meditate on them.

When you hear someone talk about an event from the Bible, be sure to read your own Bible. When you go to Sunday School, take and read your Bible. When you are in church, read your Bible!

**{Show the children the first baby picture again.}**

This is my baby picture. I'm the baby who was born into sin.

**{Show the empty frame.}**

I needed a Savior, someone who could fix my sin nature. The wages of sin is death. All have sinned and fallen short of God's glory.

I chose to believe that Jesus could make me righteous. I believed Jesus lived on earth, died, and rose again in three days. Because of this, I realized that I needed to repent, or turn away, from the sin in my heart.

Jesus is pure and perfect, and He died on the cross instead of me. I can have a righteous relationship with God the Father because He is in charge of my life now. The only reason I can go to Heaven for eternity is because God chose to **wear a costume** and be born as a human baby.

**What can we learn from the Nativity? It is important to read the Bible and know the facts about God and Jesus. Jesus is God and took the form of man. He lived on the earth and saved us from our sins.**

THE NATIVITY

# COMMENT BOX

■ ■ ■ ■ ■ ■ ■ ■ ■ ■ ■ ■ ■ ■ ■ ■ ■ ■ ■ ■

**THINK:** What went well as you taught this lesson? What can you do better?

_____
_____
_____
_____
_____
_____
_____
_____
_____

**TIP:** Always ask thinking questions as you read Scripture. We want children to think critically about Scripture and know what they believe.

# 3 JESUS AS A CHILD

■■■■■■■■■■■■■■■■■■■■■■

It is strange to think about Jesus being a little kid, but He was. There are not many verses in the Bible that tell us about His childhood, but the ones we can read are important. This lesson includes three main things that happened during Jesus' childhood.

**Scripture Reference:** Luke 2:21-52

**Materials:**

- Board to draw timeline
- Poster of Luke 2:52

**Geography:** Bethlehem, Jerusalem, Egypt, Judea, Nazareth

**Background:** Jesus was born in Bethlehem. The angels appeared to the shepherds. The shepherds went and worshiped Baby Jesus. What happened next?

JESUS AS A CHILD

# OBJECT AND BIBLE LESSON

▪▪▪▪▪▪▪▪▪▪▪▪▪▪▪▪▪▪▪▪▪▪

After Jesus was born in Bethlehem, Mary and Joseph had a visit from the shepherds.

Eight days later, Jesus was circumcised, probably in Bethlehem. This was a physical symbol of God's promise to Abraham. They then traveled to Jerusalem 33 days later to present baby Jesus to God at the temple and to offer a sacrifice of purification for Mary.

While they were there, an old man came up to them. His name was Simeon. He was a righteous man and devout to the Lord. The Holy Spirit was with him. In fact, the Holy Spirit had impressed upon Simeon's heart that he would not die until he saw the Lord's Christ. When he saw Mary and Joseph, Simeon broke out into a blessing! *"My eyes have seen Your salvation!"* he proclaimed.

During the same trip, a prophetess named Anna came up to Mary and Joseph. Anna was a widow and had dedicated her life to the Lord. She never left the temple. She served day and night. When she came up to these new parents, Anna gave thanks to God.

The Scriptures say that Mary and Joseph were amazed by all of this. Can you imagine?

Let us go through everything that has happened: **{Draw and label a timeline, if you haven't drawn it yet.}**

- An angel announced to Mary that she was going to have a baby.
- An angel told Joseph to marry Mary anyway.
- They went to Bethlehem and the baby came.
- Shepherds came to where they were, telling the parents they had come to worship their baby because an angel told them to.
- Two different strangers came up to them in a busy temple and blessed and thanked God over their baby.

Can you imagine? And that's not all!

# JESUS AS A CHILD

- The Magi visited. Jesus is referred to as a child and not a baby. Gold, frankincense, and myrrh were given.
- Then an angel appeared to Joseph again and told him to take Baby Jesus and Mary to Egypt because King Herod was going to try to kill Jesus.
- An angel appeared AGAIN and told them to return to Israel because King Herod had died.
- The family traveled back to Judah, but Joseph was told in a dream not to go there. Instead they move to a little town called Nazareth in Galilee.

After all of this, every year for Passover, Joseph, Mary, and Jesus traveled to Jerusalem for the festivities. When Jesus was 12, something different happened. When it was time to leave Jerusalem, Joseph and Mary left with a group of people, assuming Jesus was somewhere in the group. After a day's travel, they realized He was not with them. They turned around to find Jesus.

After three days, they found Jesus in the temple listening and asking the teachers questions. All who heard Him were amazed! Mary came up and asked, *"Son! Why have you treated us this way?"* Jesus replied, *"Why were you looking? Didn't you know I'd be in my Father's house?"*

Jesus liked to answer a question with a question! He did that ALL throughout His ministry.

Luke 2:52 tells us: *"And Jesus grew in wisdom, and stature, and in favor with God and man."*

**{Hold up the poster. Ask:}**

- What does it mean to grow in wisdom? [*It means not just having head knowledge, but being able to use knowledge and discernment in order to make God-pleasing decisions.*]
- What does it mean to grow in stature? [*To grow taller and older*]
- What does it mean to grow in favor, or grace, with God? [*Without faith, we cannot please God. To please God, our faith in Him must grow.*]
- What does it mean to grow in favor with man? [*To show the fruit of the Spirit on a daily basis*]

# LIFE APPLICATION

■ ■ ■ ■ ■ ■ ■ ■ ■ ■ ■ ■ ■ ■ ■ ■ ■ ■ ■ ■

No matter how old we are, we should always be striving to grow in wisdom and in favor with God and man. How can we grow in stature? We cannot change how tall we are, but we can change how healthfully we eat and how much exercise we get.

**{Ask:}**

- What can you do to grow in favor with the people around you? [*Allow for answers. We want to exhibit the fruit of the Spirit. Lead children to think of examples that display love, joy, peace, patience, kindness, goodness, faithfulness, gentleness, and self-control. Examples might include good manners, a happy attitude, and being respectful.*]

- What can you do to grow in favor with God? [*Choose Jesus to be our Master. Grow our faith. Lead children to understand that reading the Bible and then doing what it says will allow the Holy Spirit to increase our faith.*]

Jesus was a special little kid, but all kids are special. God has given each person a specific, special task to do and we do not have to wait to be grown up to do it! Children can do amazing things for God if they allow Him to work through them.

In fact, God tells people to come to Him with the faith of a child. It might be that God can use kids more than adults at times!

**What can we learn from Jesus as a child? Jesus is our example, and we should be focused on growing in wisdom and stature and in favor with God and man.**

JESUS AS A CHILD

# COMMENT BOX

■■■■■■■■■■■■■■■■■■■■

**THINK:** What went well as you taught this lesson? What can you do better?

_____

_____

_____

_____

_____

_____

_____

_____

_____

**TIP:** Everything hinges on the gospel. Help children learn that God's purpose STARTS with salvation and continues until God calls us home.

# 4 JOHN THE BAPTIST

You can tell a lot about a person by what they do. It's called fruit. In this lesson you will discuss repentance and the fruit that the Lord wants to produce in those who choose to follow Him.

**Scripture Focus:** Matthew 3 and Luke 3:1-23

**Materials:**

- Jar of honey (with honeycomb would be perfect!)
- Piece of fruit
- Poster of Luke 3:16

**Geography:** Jordan River, near Bethany

**Background:** About 30 years have gone by since Jesus was born in Bethlehem. A lot was recorded about what happened to Jesus and His family when He was born. Then there was almost silence until Jesus appeared at the Jordan River to meet His cousin.

John answered everyone,

"I baptize you with water, but there is one coming later who can do more than I can. I am not good enough to untie his sandals. He will baptize you with the Holy Spirit and with fire."

—Luke 3:16 (ICB)

JOHN THE BAPTIST

# OBJECT AND BIBLE LESSON

■■■■■■■■■■■■■■■■■■■■■■■■

**{Ask:}**

- Do you remember the facts surrounding the birth of John? [*Have the children retell the story of Zachariah, the angel, and naming the baby.*]

After Elizabeth named the baby, and Zachariah confirmed that the baby's name would be John, Zachariah could speak once more.

- What do you think his first words were? [*Allow for answers.*]

Both boys, John and Jesus, grew up.

John started preaching first. Picture what this man must have looked like. He lived out in the desert, wore camel's hair, and had a leather belt around his waist. He ate locusts and honey (Leviticus 11:22).

**{Show the jar of honey.}**

Perhaps the honey took the "crunch" out of the locusts.

Hundreds of years before John was born, the prophet Isaiah talked about a voice that would come from the wilderness. Isaiah said that the voice would have a message: *"The Lord is coming! Prepare! Make the paths straight for His coming!"*

John lived a simple life and was filled with the Holy Spirit. He started preaching in the wilderness. He had a simple message, but it was life changing: *"Repent! For the Kingdom of Heaven is at hand!"* (Prophecy fulfilled!)

**{Ask:}**

- What did he mean by the "Kingdom of Heaven"? [*Allow for answers.*]
- What does the word repent mean? [*To turn away from; to stop going one way and to choose to go another*]

*"When John the Baptist announced that the Kingdom of God was at hand, he meant that God's rule was just about to break into the world through the Messiah."* (Dr. David Naugle) So as John preached, he continued to tell the people that God was about to do something.

John was telling the people to turn away from their evil ways and to prepare themselves for the coming of the Messiah. The Lord was coming, but John did not know when. He kept preaching the same message to those who would listen.

People were convicted, and they repented of the bad things they had done. Different groups went to John and asked what they needed to do to fix their wrong choices.

To answer the crowds, John gave them specific things to do, such as: people should share possessions with those who have none; tax collectors should only tax what they ought to; and soldiers should not force people to pay them money or falsely accuse people.

People came in large numbers to be baptized by John. The Jews were familiar with individual baptism, but John's ministry was unusual because this was the first time a person baptised another. The act of baptism symbolizes the idea of dirty hearts, or souls, being made clean because of faith and repentance.

**But John knew that some people's hearts were not changed**, especially those of the Pharisees and Sadducees who came to be baptized. In fact, John called them a "*brood of vipers*"! (He called them a group of snakes!!)

The people wondered if John was the Messiah. However, John told them that One would be coming Who would baptize with the fire of the Holy Spirit, and not with water.

One day Jesus showed up at the Jordan River to be baptized. John said, "*It is I who should be baptized by You!*" Jesus told him that He needed John to baptize Him to "*fulfill all righteousness.*"

After Jesus was baptized, the heavens opened up. The Holy Spirit took on the form of a dove and flew down to Jesus. God the Father spoke from Heaven saying, "*You are My beloved Son, in You I am well-pleased.*"

This picture of Jesus in the water, with the Holy Spirit like a dove upon Him, and God's voice coming from Heaven, shows us THREE parts of God. This is called the Trinity of God.

The **Trinity** is the term we use to describe God as one God and the three persons of God: the Father, the Son, and the Holy Spirit. All three are God, but they are separate persons of God. They have different purposes.

This concept is hard to understand at times because God is God and we are human. Many times when we try to explain things about God using human terms, it does not work well.

The Trinity is something people have been studying for years. It is one of those facts about God that we can accept with faith, knowing that God is greater than what our minds can understand.

# LIFE APPLICATION

**{Hold up the piece of fruit.}**

Remember the people who were coming down to be baptized and repent, but John knew that they did not mean it? John preached about fruit. He talked about trees being cut down if they did not produce the **fruit of repentance**.

John did not mean fruit like the piece of fruit in my hand. Instead, he was talking about behavior, actions, and motivations.

Can you tell when someone is truly sorry for something bad he did to you? God can tell if you are sorry when you repent. He knows your heart.

John told those people, who did not mean to change, that the ax was waiting at the base of the tree. He added that all trees that did not bear fruit would be cut down and thrown into the fire.

**{Ask:}**

- If a tree is unhealthy, will it produce good fruit? [*No*]

If a tree is diseased, a farmer will cut it down. Not only will it not produce good fruit, but it might spread disease to other trees. John preached to these people and told them that if they did not truly repent, then they would be cut down, gotten rid of, and thrown into the fire.

Hell is a real place. People have two choices: Either believe that God's Kingdom of Heaven is attainable through Jesus, OR ignore that fact.

**{Ask:}**

- What does the fruit of repentance look like? [*Allow for answers.*]

The fruit of repentance is understanding in your heart, not just in your head, that you are a sinner and that you deserve to be cut down and thrown into the fire. The Bible tells us that because of our sin, we deserve death. (Romans 6:23)

John showed us an example of humility in Matthew 3:11. He told the people that he was not worthy of untying, or carrying, the shoes of the One to come. In the Middle East, shoes, especially the bottoms of shoes, are considered dirty.

Because of his own sin, John was expressing that he was not worthy to untie Jesus' dirty, yucky shoes.

John told us that the Kingdom of Heaven was at hand. Jesus, the Messiah, was coming. In order to recognize Jesus for Who He was, the hearts of the people—our hearts—must be prepared to *"make straight the paths of the Lord."*

The fruit of repentance is the **humble** acceptance of grace. We are not worthy to untie Jesus' shoes.

**What can we learn from John the Baptist? We need to repent, to desire to stop doing sinful things...and truly mean it in our hearts. We need to turn from doing life our own way and walk on Jesus' path of life instead.**

JOHN THE BAPTIST

# COMMENT BOX

■ ■ ■ ■ ■ ■ ■ ■ ■ ■ ■ ■ ■ ■ ■ ■ ■ ■ ■ ■ ■ ■

**THINK:** What went well as you taught this lesson? What can you do better?

_____
_____
_____
_____
_____
_____
_____
_____
_____
_____

**TIP:** Are you dealing with a sin? When preparing to teach Scripture to children, pray and ask for forgiveness so you can teach with a pure heart.

# 5 JESUS IN THE WILDERNESS

So many things in the world tempt us and our kids. There are good things that tempt and evil things that tempt. The goal is for our kids to recognize WHEN they are being tempted and then what to do about it. This fun lesson uses candy to discuss the difference between temptation and sin, and how to battle the enemy.

**Focus Scripture:** Luke 4:1-13

**Materials:**

- Package of your favorite candy (mine is M&Ms!)
- Bowl
- Poster of Luke 4:1

**Geography:** Jordan River

**Background:** The people wondered if John was the Messiah. John told them that One would be coming who would baptize with the fire of the Holy Spirit, and not with water. One day Jesus showed up at the Jordan River to be baptized. John said, *"It is I who should be baptized by You!"* But Jesus told him that He needed John to baptize Him to *"fulfill all righteousness."* After Jesus was baptized, the heavens opened up. The Holy Spirit took on the form of a dove and flew down to Jesus. God the Father spoke from Heaven saying, *"You are My beloved Son, in You I am well-pleased."*

# OBJECT AND BIBLE LESSON

**[Open the candy and pour it all into a bowl.]**

Mmmmmm...this is my favorite candy. I love to eat this candy, but because I have to teach my lesson, the bowl is going to have to sit here while I teach.

**[Look longingly at the bowl.]**

I sure do love this candy. Maybe I can have just one piece. It would not hurt anything. You would not even know I took one because there are SOOO many pieces left. But no, I said I would leave the candy alone until I was finished.

**{Read Luke 4:1-4. Ask:}**

- Who is in this story? [*Jesus and the devil*]
- What are some other names by which the devil is called? [*Satan, tempter, Lucifer, serpent, dragon, roaring lion, god of this world, adversary, etc.*]
- Where are they? [*In the wilderness*]
- What happened in the wilderness in the Old Testament? [*Lead the children to remember the 40 years of wandering of the children of Israel. Also point out that God fed them bread, or manna, from Heaven while in the desert wilderness.*]
- When did Satan tempt Jesus? [*Just after Jesus was baptized*]
- Why did Jesus go? [*He was led by the Spirit.*]
- What has happened so far? [*Jesus was baptized; He was tempted by the devil; Jesus ate nothing for 40 days; the devil told Jesus to turn stones to bread; Jesus gave an answer.*]
- How does Jesus answer? [*Jesus used Scripture.*]

**{Read Luke 4:5-8. Ask:}**

- Where are they? [*A high place, possibly Mount Hermon*]
- When did this happen? [*Just after Jesus was tempted to turn stones into bread*]
- Why did Jesus go? [*He was led by the devil. That is interesting!*]

- What did the devil do? [*He showed Jesus all of the kingdoms of the world; he told Jesus he would give Him authority over all the kingdoms if Jesus would worship him.*]

- How does Jesus answer? [*Jesus used Scripture.*]

**{Read Luke 4:9-13. Ask:}**

- Where are they? [*The highest point of the temple in Jerusalem*]

- When did this happen? [*Just after Jesus was tempted by the kingdoms of the world*]

- Why did Jesus go? [*He was led by the devil.*]

- What did the devil do? [*He asked Jesus to throw Himself off the top so the angels would catch Him; he also quoted Scripture to Jesus.*]

- How does Jesus answer? [*Jesus used Scripture.*]

# LIFE APPLICATION

**{Smell the candy.}**

Hmmm...the lesson is almost over.

**{Ask:}**

- Can I go ahead and eat one? Just one? [*No. That was not the plan. The lesson must be over.*]

We must not budge when it comes to temptation. We must do what is right.

- How did Jesus succeed? [*He quoted Scripture.*]
- Do you know of any Scriptures that I could use to help me not eat my candy during the lesson? [*Allow for answers, but lead the kids to say what Jesus said: "We shall not live by bread alone, but by every word of God."*]

Being a Jewish man, Jesus had probably memorized books and books of Scripture and was able to quote exactly the truth He needed when He needed it. The Holy Spirit was able to bring to His mind what He needed for strength. And what is so amazing is that we have this same help when WE need it!

**{Ask:}**

- How much Scripture do you have memorized? [*Allow for answers, but lead the children to recognize that MANY different types of situations can use the same Scriptures. However, if they do not have it memorized, then the Holy Spirit will not have anything to work with. They will not be able to have the Scripture come to their minds if it is not hidden in their hearts.*]

Once you have faith in Jesus and live totally for Him, the Holy Spirit lives inside of you. Whenever you need help, the Holy Spirit is waiting for you. He wants to guide you when you make decisions. He wants to help you make good choices. He wants to give you kind words to say and good deeds to do.

If you are reading your Bible, memorizing Scripture, and thinking about how God can use that Scripture in your life, then you are giving the Holy Spirit weapons against the evil one.

Satan wants you to fail. He wanted Jesus to bow down to him. Because Jesus beat the devil and rose from the grave, Satan has no power over you...IF you believe in Jesus AND know His Word.

**{Ask:}**

- Did Jesus sin when He was tempted? [*No*]

The temptation itself is not the sin. **Sin is the ACT of giving in to the temptation.** Temptation always looks good.

**{Show the candy. Ask:}**

- Am I sinning by holding the bowl? [*No*]
- Am I sinning by talking about eating the candy? [*No*]

**{Pick up a piece of candy. Ask:}**

- Am I sinning by holding the piece of candy? [*No*]
- Am I being tempted? [*Yes*]
- What would I have to do to sin? [*Eat the piece of candy*]
- Is eating candy sinful? [*No*]
- So why would my eating THIS candy be sinful? [*Allow for answers. Guide the children to see that eating the candy would go against what you said you were going to do at the beginning. You would be untrustworthy because you did not do what you said you were going to do.*]
- If I were to sit here and eat this entire bowl of candy, what would happen? [*I would get sick, gain weight, and be a glutton (someone who eats too much out of greed).*]
- What does sin do? [*Allow for answers. It hurts those who sin and hurts those around the sinner.*]

Sin can look nice, fancy, fun, and exciting. That is why it is tempting...but in truth, sin is evil and goes against the heart of God.

**What can we learn from Jesus in the wilderness? Prepare for the battle with Satan by reading and memorizing Scripture. Then when temptation is in your face, call on the Holy Spirit. He will be waiting for you.**

# COMMENT BOX

**THINK:** What went well as you taught this lesson? What can you do better?

_____
_____
_____
_____
_____
_____
_____
_____
_____
_____

**TIP:** After the lesson, enjoy a piece of candy and share with the children.

# 6 JESUS CALLS THE TWELVE DISCIPLES

## ■■■■■■■■■■■■■■■■■■■■■

What does it mean to be a disciple? Who were Jesus' first disciples? Use a fishing rod and net to teach children about the first disciples and how disciples today can work together to fish for men.

**Scripture Focus:** Matthew 4:17-22; Mark 1:16-20, 2:13-17; Luke 5:1-11, 27-32; John 1:35-51

**Materials:**

- Fishing rod
- Fishing net
- Poster of Mark 1:17

**Geography:** Galilee, Capernaum

**Background:** During Passover, Jesus went into the temple court and drove out the animals and the money changers. A few days later, Jesus had a remarkable conversation with Nicodemus. This conversation included the words of John 3:16. Just before and during this time period, Jesus asked some men to follow Him.

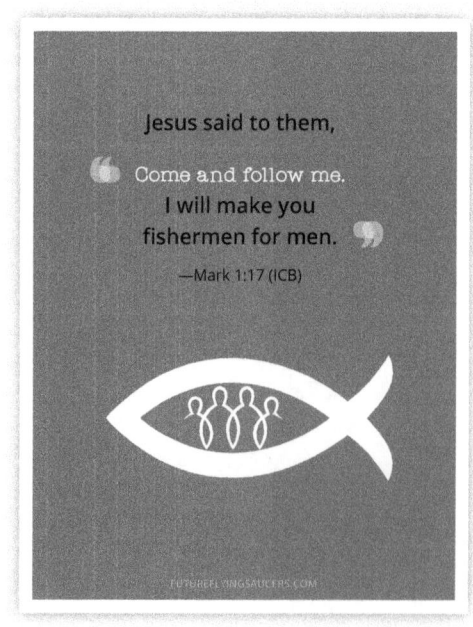

Jesus said to them,

" Come and follow me. I will make you fishermen for men. "

—Mark 1:17 (ICB)

JESUS CALLS THE TWELVE DISCIPLES

# OBJECT AND BIBLE LESSON

**{Hold up the fishing rod. Ask:}**

- What is this? [*A fishing rod*]
- What do you do with it? [*Catch fish*]
- How many people can use a fishing rod at one time? [*One*]
- How many fish can you catch at one time? [*One*]

**{Put the fishing pole to the side. You will use it later.}**

After Jesus went into the wilderness, John the Baptist started having trouble with the Pharisees and with King Herod. After Jesus returned from the wilderness, He went back to the Jordan where John was ministering. John had disciples that followed him. One day John saw Jesus, and he told two of his disciples about Jesus. Those two disciples stopped following John and started following Jesus.

In fact, they literally left John and followed Jesus. Jesus stopped and asked them what they wanted. The men told Jesus they wanted to follow Him, so He took them to where He was living and they stayed with Him. One of the disciples was a man named Andrew. The other was John (not John the Baptist). After meeting Jesus, Andrew went to get his brother, Simon. When Simon came to Jesus, Jesus changed Simon's name to Peter, which means "rock." Obviously, Jesus knew something about Peter that Peter knew nothing of, because changing someone's name is a BIG deal.

At some point after this, John the Baptist was arrested and put in jail. Jesus was teaching, and more and more people were following Him. One day Jesus was teaching at the Sea of Galilee. He asked the fishermen (Peter and Andrew, the brothers) to push out their boat and allow Him to teach by boat. Once the crowds went away, Jesus told the men to throw out their nets.

**{Hold up the fishing net.}**

This is similar to what the men had, only theirs would have been much bigger. The men told Jesus, *"We fished all night and caught nothing."* Jesus told them to throw the nets out again.

Peter and Andrew threw out the nets and WOW! Did they catch fish! They called out to their friends, James and John, who were in another boat, to come and help because their nets were breaking! Both of the boats were filled with fish, and they began to sink. Peter, because of his amazement, fell before Jesus and said, *"Get away from me, Lord. I am a sinful man."* Jesus replied back saying, *"Have no fear. You will be catching men from now on."*

**{Hold the net up again.}**

- How many people can use this net? [*More than one*]
- How many fish can this net hold? [*A large number*]

While in Galilee, Jesus found a few more who chose to follow Him. He found Philip, who then found Nathanael, or Bartholomew. Under a fig tree, Philip told Bartholomew about Jesus, and he responded, *"Can anything good come out of Nazareth?"* Philip told him to come and see. When Bartholomew met Jesus, he realized that Jesus knew about him. Bartholomew asked, *"How do you know me?"* and Jesus replied, *"Before Philip called you, I saw you under the fig tree."* Do you realize that Jesus knows EVERYTHING about you? Jesus knows what you think, say, and do!

After performing a miracle, Jesus walked in the area of Galilee and passed a tax collector name Levi, or Matthew. Jesus told Matthew, *"Follow me,"* and Matthew did. Later, Matthew held a reception at his home for Jesus and "sinners" came to the party. The Pharisees did not like this. Jesus told them, *"A doctor does not take care of people who are healthy. He helps those who are sick."* That is what Jesus does. He helps sinners, especially those who realize they are sinners.

Many people followed Jesus. Jesus selected 12 men out of the large group. They are known as the "disciples." He appointed His disciples to be with Him. Jesus also sent them out to preach and gave them authority to cast out demons.

**Here is a way to remember the names of the 12 disciples:**

**Five *J*s {Hold up five fingers of one hand. Point to each finger as you say a name.}**

- Judas Iscariot, Judas Thaddeus, John, James, and James the Less

**BAM {Have your fingers make a *W* by holding up three fingers. All of these names end in *W*. The first letter of each name spells BAM.}**

- Bartholomew, Andrew, and Matthew

**Final Four {In American basketball playoffs, the last four games are referred to as the "Final Four," and players score points, or "PPTS." There are four disciples left and their names begin with the letters P, P, T, and S.}**

- Peter, Philip, Thomas, and Simon

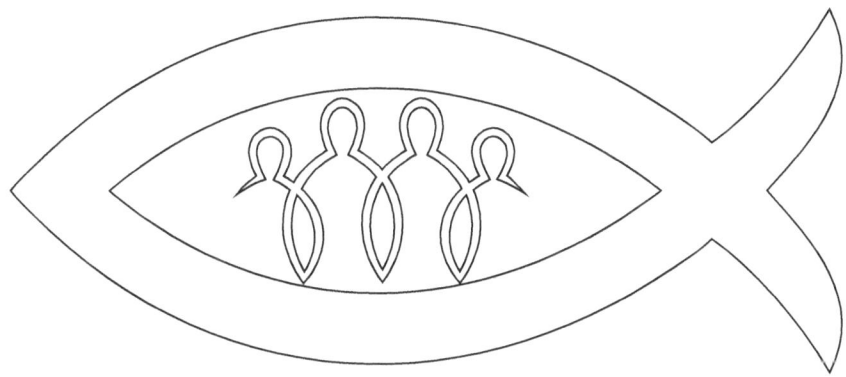

# LIFE APPLICATION

**{Show the fishing rod once more. Ask:}**

- How many people can fish with this? How many fish can be caught? [*One; one*]

**{Hold up the net.}**

THIS is how Jesus wants us to fish. Jesus selected 12 men who He knew would change the world. He chose each one for a specific reason, with certain talents and abilities. Each disciple had a purpose. The church works the same way. Each person, including YOU, has a purpose. You have talents and abilities to do jobs that only YOU can do for God. It is like everyone in the church has a piece of the large net, and everyone is working together to be fishers of men.

**{Ask:}**

- What happens when one person does not do what he/she is supposed to do for God? [*Perhaps part of the net drops.*]
- What can happen if someone drops the net? [*Fish can escape.*]

Therefore, if someone chooses to disobey the Lord by not using his or her talents to work in the Kingdom, then that person will miss out on catching people for the Lord.

Are you holding up your part of the net?

**What can we learn from Jesus calling the 12 disciples? Following Jesus means that our focus changes. We stop what we are doing, we choose to live like Jesus, and then we work as a team to tell others about Jesus.**

JESUS CALLS THE TWELVE DISCIPLES

# COMMENT BOX

■ ■ ■ ■ ■ ■ ■ ■ ■ ■ ■ ■ ■ ■ ■ ■ ■ ■ ■ ■

**THINK:** What went well as you taught this lesson? What can you do better?

_____
_____
_____
_____
_____
_____
_____
_____
_____

**TIP:** Ask questions as you read. Be sure to explain any vocabulary words that children might not know.

# 7 JESUS' FIRST MIRACLES

Who was Jesus and how do we know? Was He really God's Son? This lesson will help children understand that Jesus has power over nature and sickness just as God the Father does.

**Scripture Focus:** John 2:1-11, 4:46-54

**Materials:**

- Wedding veil (If you don't have a veil, use wedding pictures.)
- Poster of John 2:11

**Geography:** Galilee, Cana

**Background:** Jesus went to John to be baptized. He then went into the wilderness. After that, Jesus called some disciples. Two of John's disciples went to Jesus and asked to follow Him. One was Andrew. Andrew went and got his brother Simon and introduced him to Jesus. Jesus then called Philip and Nathanael.

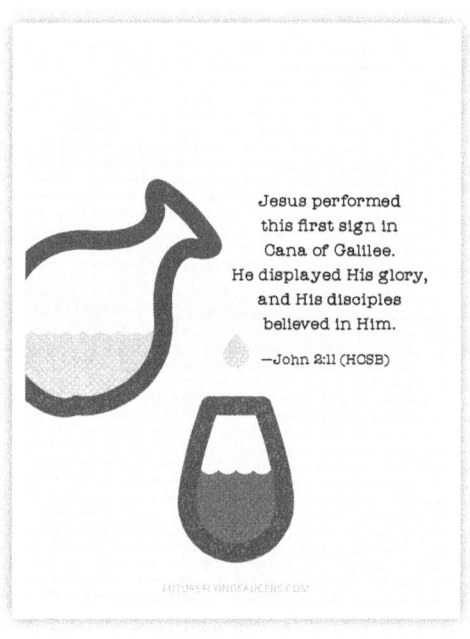

Jesus performed this first sign in Cana of Galilee. He displayed His glory, and His disciples believed in Him.

—John 2:11 (HCSB)

# OBJECT AND BIBLE LESSON

■ ■ ■ ■ ■ ■ ■ ■ ■ ■ ■ ■ ■ ■ ■ ■ ■ ■ ■ ■ ■ ■ ■

**{Hold up the veil or wedding pictures. Ask:}**

- Have you ever been to, or been in, a wedding? [*Allow for answers. Allow the children to describe their experiences, and ask questions about what happened during the ceremonies and the receptions. Through this conversation, establish the local marriage tradition.*]

Weddings are beautiful!

**{Describe some local wedding traditions and then talk about unusual traditions you have seen when going to a wedding. Ask:}**

- Sometimes people do unusual things. I've told you some unusual wedding traditions. What would it take for you to believe something that is unusual? [*Allow for answers, such as seeing with your own eyes or hearing the story from a person you trust.*]

It is interesting that Jesus' first miracle happens at a wedding, because in future conversations, Jesus will mention how He is the bridegroom and the church is the bride.

There was a wedding in Cana. Mary, Jesus' mother, and Jesus and His disciples were at the wedding feast. This would be like a wedding reception, only these feasts would last up to seven days. Usually all of the best food and drink would be served the first few days to the guests, and then as the feast went on, the food and drink would not be of the best quality.

At this wedding, the host ran out of wine. Mary somehow found out and told Jesus. He responded to her, *"What does this have to do with me? My hour has not yet come."* This was during the time when Jesus' ministry was still beginning, but Mary told the servants to do whatever Jesus told them.

There were six stone water pots. They were large enough to hold 20-30 gallons each. These particular pots were used for the Jewish custom of purification. Before eating, Jews would wash their hands, along with the cooking and eating utensils. There were probably a lot of guests, so large jars of water would be needed.

Jesus told the servants to fill the jars to the brim—ALL the way up to the top. Then He told the servants to take some out and take it to the headwaiter. **Jesus did not touch the pots...**

### {Ask:}

- Who was at the wedding? [*Jesus, Mary, the disciples, guests, servants, master of the feast, bridegroom (and possibly the bride)*]

- What happened? [*The wine ran out at the wedding. Mary told the servants to do whatever Jesus said to do. He told them to fill the large jars with water.*]

- Why do you think Jesus said to His mother that His "hour had not come"? [*Perhaps it was not time for Jesus to reveal Who He was.*]

The water changed to wine. In fact, the master of the feast went to the groom and complimented him, telling him that he had saved the best wine until the END of the feast. Scripture tells us that the master of the feast did not know what Jesus did. The servants knew what had happened and so did the disciples. The Bible tells us that with this miracle, Jesus showed His glory and the disciples believed in Him. **This shows us that Jesus is the Creator and has power over nature.**

Jesus traveled to Jerusalem for Passover. While there, Jesus had a conversation with Nicodemus. He then traveled to Samaria where he spoke with a woman by a well. Then He went back to Cana.

### {Read John 4:46-54.}

- What do we know about the man who came to Jesus? [*He was a nobleman, or royal official; his son was sick to the point of death in Capernaum; he had heard Jesus was in the area; he implored, or begged, for Jesus to heal his son.*]

A royal official came to Jesus. We are not told who this was, but it was probably someone in Herod's government. The fact that this high-ranking official came to Jesus should not be missed. Even though this event is early in Jesus' ministry, He was already beginning to be a controversial figure in Israel. This official possibly risked his reputation and future job by going to Jesus. For this father, his son was most important. This official begged Jesus to come with him and heal his sick son, for he was close to death. Jesus replied, *"Unless you people see signs and wonders you will not believe."*

Why did He say this? Jesus was suggesting that the leaders, including the father, would not believe in Him apart from the working of miracles. Look at what Jesus does...

# JESUS' FIRST MIRACLES

The official begged again for Jesus to come. Jesus told the man, *"Go, your son lives."* At this point the father could either believe Jesus without seeing a miracle, or choose to not believe. Scripture tells us that the man believed. That is what Jesus wants from us. He wants us to have faith in Him without seeing miracles.

The official's servants met him on the way home and told him that his son was well. In fact, they told him the specific time that the boy was healed. The official knew that it matched the time when he had spoken to Jesus. I am sure this miracle caused the father's faith to grow! **This shows us Jesus had power over sickness and that He did not have to be with a person to heal.**

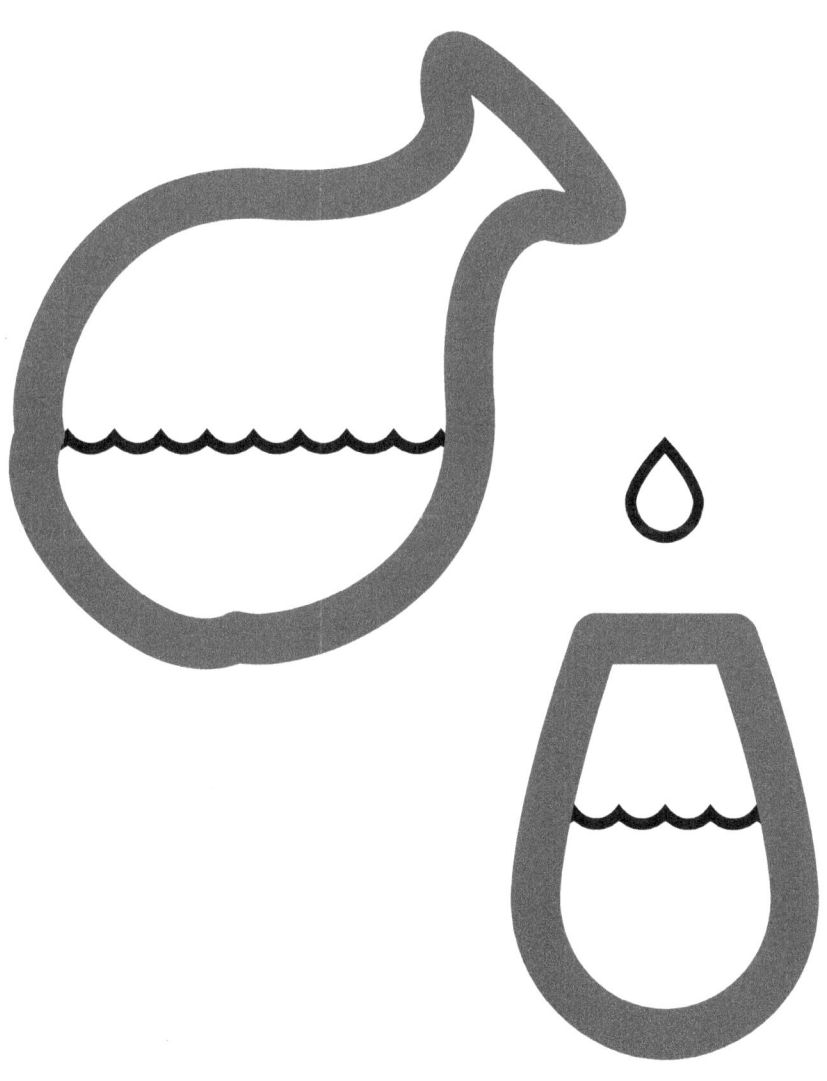

# LIFE APPLICATION

**{Hold up the veil.}**

Both of Jesus' first miracles in the book of John took place in the same town. First, a wedding groom was saved from an embarrassing situation when the water was turned to wine. Second, a government official's son was healed. One result from the first miracle was that the disciples who were there believed in Jesus. A result from the second miracle was that the official and his whole household believed in Jesus. The first miracle was sort of in secret, or at least with a smaller crowd. The second miracle was public.

Jesus did exactly what was needed in each situation so the people involved would believe in Him. There were some Jews who wanted Him to perform miracles in front of them before they believed who He was. **That is not faith.**

Faith is believing in things hoped for. The official believed Jesus in faith. The official hoped with his entire being that Jesus had spoken the truth. THEN when he saw his son alive, the official's belief was solidified, along with that of his whole household.

Are you in a situation where you need Jesus to work a miracle? Check your faith. Are you wanting to see the miracle BEFORE you believe? Faith is believing in Jesus and in Who He is even if the miracle never comes.

**What can we learn from the wedding in Cana and the healing of the nobleman's son? Jesus is God. He has power over nature and sickness. Jesus also knows our heart and can see our level of faith. He will do exactly what needs to be done at the right time.**

# COMMENT BOX

**THINK:** What went well as you taught this lesson? What can you do better?

_____
_____
_____
_____
_____
_____
_____
_____
_____

**TIP:** Faith can be a complicated topic to teach because it is not tangible and it is hard to describe. Even our ability for faith comes from God. Try to point out the faith, or lack of faith, of Bible characters as examples.

# 8 JESUS AND NICODEMUS

The Pharisee was confused. After all, Jesus was teaching new ideas with authority. Use this simple but profound lesson to teach the truth of being born again.

**Scripture Focus:** John 3:1-21

**Materials:**

- Candles (I used electric votive candles.)
- Bowl of water (I used this for my personal testimony, but you can use the concept.)
- Poster of John 3:16

**Geography:** Jerusalem

**Background:** After Jesus was baptized, the heavens opened up. The Holy Spirit took on the form of a dove and flew down to Jesus. God the Father spoke from Heaven saying, *"You are My beloved Son, in You I am well-pleased."* The Spirit then led Jesus into the wilderness where Jesus was tempted by Satan. Jesus then began His ministry, found disciples for His inner circle, and started doing miracles.

# OBJECT AND BIBLE LESSON

**{Have the candles lit and the lights off before the children enter the room.}**

The event we are going to hear about today took place at night, but first I want to tell you about something Jesus did a few days earlier.

Jesus was in Jerusalem. It was time for the Passover celebration. Jerusalem would have been packed with people from the surrounding countries. Jesus went to the temple, and in the outer area He found many tables with money changers and people selling animals for sacrifices. Jesus found the materials to make a whip, and He began to drive out the money changers and the animals from the temple. He also overturned the tables. Jesus told the people selling doves, *"Take these things away! Do not make my Father's house a house of business!"* (John 2:13-16)

**{Ask:}**

- Why would Jesus be so upset? What was the purpose of the temple? [*The temple was a place of worship. It is also possible that the business people were taking advantage of, or cheating, those who were visiting for Passover.*]

The Jews were not happy with Jesus. *"By what authority do you do these things?"* they asked. Jesus responded, *"Destroy this temple and in three days I will raise it up."*

**{Ask:}**

- What do you think Jesus talking about? [*His death on the cross and resurrection*]
- What did the Jews think He meant? [*The temple building*]

**{Whisper}**

One night, a man named Nicodemus came to Jesus. Nicodemus was a Pharisee and a leader of the Sanhedrin. Jesus and Nicodemus had an interesting conversation. We do not know why Nicodemus came to Jesus at night. Maybe he had a busy day. Perhaps he wanted to see Jesus without all of the people around Him. Maybe Nicodemus did not want other people to see HIM talking to Jesus.

# JESUS AND NICODEMUS

Whatever the reason, Jesus and Nicodemus had one of the most important conversations of all time.

**{Read through John 3:1-21, preferably from the International Children's Bible.}**

**After Verse 2:**

Many times, Jesus ignores the question or comment from the person speaking to Him and goes straight to the person's heart issue. Nicodemus had been watching Jesus do miracles and drive the money changers out. He knew that Jesus was someone different. *MAYBE* he thought that Jesus might be the Messiah.

**After Verse 7:**

Nicodemus knew that Jesus did not literally mean he needed to be born from his mother again. What Jesus was telling him was new.

Jesus was telling Nicodemus that he needed to experience a birth of his spirit. A sinful person cannot be born of the Spirit on their own. A person is literally born of water through an earthly mother. People are born of the Spirit through Jesus. If a person is not born of the Spirit, then he may not enter the Kingdom of God.

**After Verse 21:**

Wasn't that a strange conversation?

- Did you recognize some words in those verses? [*John 3:16*]

John 3:16, one of the most recognizable verses from Scripture, comes from the conversation with Nicodemus. Here was a man who knew the Scriptures. He had dedicated his entire life to learning and interpreting the words of God. He probably had books of the Old Testament memorized.

One of the things Jesus told Nicodemus was that people testify, or witness, or tell people about what they know and experience—what they see, hear, feel, taste, and smell. Jesus explained that if Nicodemus was not willing to believe what he heard Jesus saying, then why would he believe Jesus if He told him things of Heaven? Nicodemus could not see Heaven or experience it without being born of the Spirit. Then Jesus told Nicodemus the most quoted Bible verse, telling him exactly how to experience eternal life.

A person has to be born again, or born of the Spirit. Through faith in Jesus, the Holy Spirit washes you clean, and as a result, you live differently. You live in the Spirit. Once you do that, then you can experience the Kingdom of God.

# LIFE APPLICATION

■■■■■■■■■■■■■■■■■■■■■

**{This is a great time to share either your salvation testimony or some other time when you experienced God do something in you. Here is my testimony. You are welcome to use it as a story, or use your own testimony.}**

When I was a child, I was filled with Bible knowledge, much like Nicodemus. He knew a lot more than me. But for a girl growing up in church, I knew a lot. I knew most of the stories of the Bible. I would win all of the Bible drills. I could recite the books of the Bible.

That is all it was. It was head knowledge. None of it had touched my heart, my soul. Then one night when I was in seventh grade, there were some people talking about Jesus at my church. Something was different. Something gripped me on the inside.

I knew I was not right on the inside. I looked like a good church girl on the outside, but I knew I was sinful on the inside. I remembered that sin is anything that I think, do, or say that does not please God.

**{Bring out the bowl of water.}**

A man talked about how my heart was dirty with sin and that there was nothing I could do to wash the sin away. However, IF I believed that Jesus was real and that He was born, died on the cross, and came back to life three days later, THEN I would be born again. I had to have faith in Jesus. JESUS would be the One to wash my sin away.

He also talked about feeling sorry for the wrong things I had done. He said that my sin made me guilty, and that I had wronged God. God is holy and perfect. I am not. Because of my sin, I deserved God's wrath and anger. I deserved death. I deserved to be put away from God forever.

When I chose to believe in Christ and KNEW He was my Savior, it was like Jesus took my heart and washed it with the water of the Spirit. My heart was changed. I had been transformed! I KNEW it!! I had experienced the saving power of God, and I will never be the same again. Scripture says that once you choose to follow Jesus, you become a new creation. Jesus took God's wrath for me upon Himself when He died on the cross. He was separated from God instead of me.

**{Put your hands in the water and "wash" them.}**

Just as you can wash your hands free from dirt, Jesus can wash your sinful heart and make you righteous. When you do this, you are born again. You get the righteousness of Jesus.

You do not go back inside your mom and go through the birthing process again.

Instead, your soul is made new, or born again, of the Spirit. You become a new creation. You are transformed on the inside.

Once you are made clean, you should not want to return to a sinful heart. Instead, you will want to read the Bible and find out everything you can do to live a life worthy of Jesus.

Once Jesus saves you, you will want to tell everyone around you what He did. You do this by being baptized and confessing, or telling people, with your mouth that Jesus is now your Lord.

**{Ask:}**

- When we are born again, will we stop sinning? [*No. We still have our sin nature inside us, but we can now ask God to forgive us for our sins, and God gives us grace. We should try to not sin.*]
- If we sin, do we have to be born again all over again? [*No. Once we are born again, and we seriously are choosing to have Jesus as our Master, then we try hard to not sin. But when we do fail, we can go straight to God, ask for forgiveness, and receive that forgiveness. Through this process, God transforms us into the image of Jesus.*]

**What can we learn from Jesus and Nicodemus? God loves the world so much that He was willing to send Jesus, His Son, to die for our sins so that we might be born again.**

# COMMENT BOX

**THINK:** What went well as you taught this lesson? What can you do better?

_____
_____
_____
_____
_____
_____
_____
_____
_____

**TIP:** Once a child shows faith in Jesus, he is ready to be discipled. Use the book *Walk This Way: Ethics and Sanctification Lessons for Kids* (https://www.futureflyingsaucers.com/walk-this-way-ethics-and-sanctification-lessons-for-kids) and/or the book *Mateo's Choice* (https://www.futureflyingsaucers.com/mateos-choice) for help in discipling children.

# 9 THE WOMAN AT THE WELL

Jesus was unconventional while He was here on earth. One event included speaking to the Samaritan woman at the well. Why did Jesus do this? Use a glass of water to teach children about the Living Water.

**Scripture Focus:** John 4:1-42

**Materials:**

- Glass of water
- Poster of John 4:14

**Geography:** Samaria, Sychar, Judea, Galilee

**Background:** Jesus selected 12 men called "disciples" to mentor and prepare for ministry. Jesus and Nicodemus had an amazing conversation about a second birth. Jesus decided to go to Galilee through Samaria.

Samaria is where the Samaritans lived. This was a group of people who were hated by the Jews, but Jesus disagreed with this.

THE WOMAN AT THE WELL

# OBJECT AND BIBLE LESSON

■ ■ ■ ■ ■ ■ ■ ■ ■ ■ ■ ■ ■ ■ ■ ■ ■ ■ ■ ■ ■

**{Hold up the glass of water. Ask:}**

- What is this? [*A glass of water*]
- When do you like to drink water? [*When thirsty, on a hot day, after playing*]
- After you drink, are you ever thirsty again? [*Yes*]
- How come? [*Allow for answers. The science behind why we become thirsty has to do with the fact that water escapes our bodies in many ways and must be replenished if we are to live.*]

After the Passover, Jesus started having some issues with the Pharisees, so He decided to leave the area of Judah and go back to Galilee. He went through an area called Samaria.

Samaria was a country filled with people that the Jews considered half-breeds because of mixed marriages between Jews and people who were transported to Israel by the Assyrians. These were people who were brought to the area during the years of exile.

When Nehemiah returned to rebuild the temple after the exile, Samaritans offered to help. They were turned down, and they became hostile. Over the years, the relationship between Jews and Samaritans became volatile. The Samaritans were not allowed to sacrifice in the Jewish temple, and Jews would walk around the area of Samaria, traveling many miles out of the way.

Not Jesus. He went through the area to Jacob's Well in Sychar. There He met a woman.

The location of this well is important. Not too far from Sychar used to be an area called Shechem. In the Old Testament we learn that God appeared to Abram at Shechem and gave Him the Covenant Promises. One of those promises was that all of the world would be blessed through Abraham. Shechem became a place of worship. These promises were handed down to Abram's son Isaac and to his son, Jacob. Jacob bought this land and dug the well where Jesus met this woman.

# THE WOMAN AT THE WELL

This woman had a history of sin just like you and I do. The disciples went into town for food, and when this woman came to the well, Jesus asked her for some water. This took her by surprise!

Why?

Jesus was a Jew.

**{When you dramatize this encounter, change your voice and shift your body from left to right as each person speaks in turn. Consider showing appropriate facial expressions for the woman. Hold the water glass while you are acting.}**

Let's listen to this conversation:

Woman: You, a Jew, are asking me, a Samaritan, for water?

*Jesus: If you knew who I was, you'd ask me for living water.*

Woman: You have no bucket and the well is deep. Where do you get this living water? Are you greater than Jacob? He gave us this well.

*Jesus: If you drink this water, you will be thirsty again. If you drink the water I give you, then you will never be thirsty again. The water I give becomes a spring and will well up to eternal life.*

Woman: I want some of this living water! I don't want to have to come and draw water again.

*Jesus: Go get your husband.*

Woman: I don't have a husband.

*Jesus: You are right. In fact, you have had five husbands and the man you are with now is not your husband.*

Woman: Sir, I think you are a prophet.

The woman then proceeded to change the subject and asked Jesus where people should worship God. In Samaria? or only in Jerusalem? He responded that the time had come for people to worship in spirit and in truth and that it didn't matter where one worshiped.

Then an amazing thing happened. The woman said, *"I know that the Messiah is coming."* Jesus responded, *"I am He."*

The fact that Jesus revealed who He was to a Samaritan woman is important.

It is important because it shows that **Jesus valued women**. She was also a Samaritan, which teaches us that **Jesus values ALL people, no matter their culture**. She was also a woman who had had five husbands. This teaches us that **Jesus values people no matter what sin they have in life**.

But there is an even more important reason why Jesus said this. Remember the promise given to Abram? God has said all of the nations would be blessed by him. This was a promise of the coming Messiah. At this well, near the location where God made His promise to Abram, Jesus revealed that He was the Messiah who fulfilled God's promise.

The disciples returned to Jesus and were amazed to find Him speaking to this woman. The woman left her water jar, ran to town, and said, *"Come meet the man who has told me everything I have ever done. Can this be the Christ?"* The whole town went out to meet Jesus.

THE WOMAN AT THE WELL

# LIFE APPLICATION

**{Hold up the glass of water.}**

The whole town came out to meet Jesus. One woman shared her testimony, or her story, and many in the town believed in Jesus.

**{Use fingers to flick water onto the children. The children will giggle! Do not hit them in the face, though—at least, not on purpose!}**

This is what happens when you share your Jesus story. When you meet Jesus, you cannot help it! You tell others about what happened! The Living Water that is in you will spread onto the person you tell. They may or may not choose to follow Jesus, but you shared the Living Water with them.

When the disciples came back to Jesus, they tried to get Him to eat food, but He refused. He said, *"My food is to do the will of God."* He told the disciples to lift up their eyes, because the fields were white with harvest.

In other words, the people of the town were on their way. They were ready to hear what Jesus had to say. That woman told her Jesus story, and the people came running to hear the gospel.

Jesus is the Living Water. As people believed, they then went to others and told their Jesus story.

**{Flick the water again.}**

The living water bubbled over and spread. If you are not telling other people your Jesus story, then you are not spreading the Living Water. Allow His Living Water to bubble out of you!

**What can we learn from the woman at the well? We must have faith in Jesus so we can have Living Water to share with others. That Living Water gives us, and others, eternal life.**

THE WOMAN AT THE WELL

# COMMENT BOX

■ ■ ■ ■ ■ ■ ■ ■ ■ ■ ■ ■ ■ ■ ■ ■ ■ ■ ■ ■ ■

**THINK:** What went well as you taught this lesson? What can you do better?

_____
_____
_____
_____
_____
_____
_____
_____
_____
_____

**TIP:** For Old Testament history object lessons, use the book *What God is Doing: Old Testament Object Lessons for Kids* (https://www.futureflyingsaucers.com/what-god-is-doing-book).

# 10 JESUS HEALS THE LAME MAN

■■■■■■■■■■■■■■■■■■■■■■

When a person encounters Jesus, that person can either believe Jesus is Who He says He is, or choose not to believe. This object lesson exemplifies this truth. Use a bowl of water to act out the event and discuss what Jesus is saying to us.

**Scripture Focus:** John 5:1-18

**Materials:**

- Large bowl of water
- 2 volunteers
- Poster of John 5:9

**Geography:** Jerusalem

**Background:** There was a wedding in Cana. Mary, Jesus' mother, and Jesus and His disciples were at the wedding feast. Jesus turned the water into wine. A royal official came to Jesus. This official begged Jesus to come with him and heal his sick son, for he was close to death. Jesus did not go with the official. Instead, Jesus told the man, *"Go, your son lives."* The official's servants met him on the way home and told him that his son was well.

> the man was well. He picked up his mat and started walking. The day all this happened was a Sabbath day.
>
> —John 5:9 (ESV)

# OBJECT LESSON

■ ■ ■ ■ ■ ■ ■ ■ ■ ■ ■ ■ ■ ■ ■ ■ ■ ■ ■ ■ ■ ■ ■

**{Choose a volunteer. Have him come up front and sit on the floor. Designate the child as unable to walk, or "lame." Put the bowl of water a distance away, far enough that he cannot reach it when stretched out. Explain that IF the water moves, he must somehow get to the bowl and put his hand in the water before the water is still again. However, he cannot use his legs. Gently shake the bowl. Allow the child to attempt to get to you. Make sure the water is still quickly. Do this two or three times. This will be silly, but the point will be made that the lame man was not able to reach the water in time.}**

So sorry!! You cannot seem to reach the water before it is still again! I guess you will not get healed this time. Let us see what Jesus did.

**{Have the volunteer stay where he is.}**

Jesus left Cana and went back to Jerusalem for a feast. While there, Jesus went near the pool of Bethesda.

The book of John tells us that if the waters were stirred up, then the first person into the pool would be healed. Therefore, many people with different ailments would sit for extended periods of time waiting for the waters to be stirred. Archeologists think they have found this pool; it must have been thought to have healing powers, because the Romans built baths on top of this ritual pool.

**{Choose someone to be Jesus and ask the question of the lame man. Guide the children through the dialogue so everyone hears the words again.}**

Jesus walked by the pool and noticed a lame man. He had been lame for 38 years. Jesus asked the man, *"Do you want to be healed?"* The man responded that he had no one to help him into the pool when it was stirred. Someone would always get there ahead of him.

Jesus replied, *"Take up your bed and walk."* The man did just as Jesus said.

**{Have the "lame" man pretend to roll up his bed. Ask:}**

- What do you think the lame man was feeling after being healed? [*Allow for answers.*]

# JESUS HEALS THE LAME MAN

This healing happened on the Sabbath. Some Jewish leaders saw the man carrying his bed. This was against the rules of the Sabbath. Carrying something is considered work, and a good Jew did not work on the Sabbath.

The leaders told the man that carrying his bed was unlawful. The man replied, *"The man who healed me said to pick up the bed and walk. And so I did."* They then asked who it was who healed him. The former lame man did not know, because Jesus had withdrawn back into the crowds.

Later, Jesus found the formerly lame man in the temple and said, *"See, you are well! Do not sin anymore, so nothing worse will happen to you."* Then the man went and told the Jewish leaders that it had been Jesus Who healed him.

After this, the Jewish leaders persecuted Jesus and desired to kill Him because Jesus was doing these things on the Sabbath. Jesus responded back to them by saying, *"My Father is working, so I am working."* The Jews wanted to seek out a way to kill Jesus because He called God His Father. Jesus had made Himself equal with God.

# LIFE APPLICATION

**{Hold up the bowl of water.}**

- Where did the healing come from? The water? Or Jesus? [*Jesus*]
- Did the lame man ask to be healed? [*No*]
- Why do you think Jesus healed the man? [*Allow for answers.*]

Jesus has power over disease and sickness. What is interesting about this event is that the lame man did not ask for healing. We do not know if he believed in Jesus or even knew who He was. Jesus healed him anyway. The Scriptures tell us that Jesus knew the man had been lame for 38 years. It is nice to know that God knows how long you have suffered!

- Did Jesus ever do anything wrong? [*No*]
- Who was wrong in this event? [*The Jewish leaders*]
- What were they doing that was wrong? [*Allow for answers. Lead the children to understand that making a lot of laws and obeying them does not make a person righteous. The Jews had made the following of laws more important than helping people in need.*]

Jesus is perfect. He did not do anything wrong by healing on the Sabbath as the Jewish leaders claimed. The Jewish leaders had so many laws that they tried to regulate and enforce, that they themselves could not keep them all. However, they were quick to point out the failures of others and ignore their own.

In another conversation Jesus pointed out that the Sabbath was made for man. The Ten Commandments were given to man. God did not need them. Man needed them.

- Have you ever done anything wrong? [*Yes*]
- Which of the Ten Commandments have you broken? [*Allow for answers.*]

The Bible tells us that when we break one of the laws, then we are guilty of breaking all of them. When we break one of the laws, then we sin. The Bible tells us that, because of our sin, we deserve to die and have no relationship with God.

God sent Jesus to the earth to die on the cross. When He was on the cross, He took all of our sins (past, present, and future) upon Himself. When He died, our sins died with Him. He took our place. We are given the righteousness of Jesus if we have faith in Him.

However, Jesus did not stay dead, because He is God. He has power over death, just like He has power over disease.

That lame man did nothing to earn his healing. Jesus chose to heal the man because He loved him.

There is nothing you can do to earn a right relationship with God. What you can do is realize that you are a sinner and that Jesus took your sins upon Himself and died instead of your dying. It is having faith in Jesus Christ that makes you righteous. Not laws, but Jesus.

**What can we learn from Jesus healing the lame man? Jesus told the lame man to sin no more. He also told the Jews that He was equal with God the Father. Only God can forgive sins. Only the Son of God can be equal to God. Jesus wants us to know that He is God in the flesh. Immanuel. Only He can make us righteous before God.**

JESUS HEALS THE LAME MAN

# COMMENT BOX

■ ■ ■ ■ ■ ■ ■ ■ ■ ■ ■ ■ ■ ■ ■ ■ ■ ■ ■ ■ ■ ■

**THINK:** What went well as you taught this lesson? What can you do better?

_____
_____
_____
_____
_____
_____
_____
_____
_____
_____

**TIP:** This is a great event to dramatize depending upon the number of children you teach. Add in Jewish leaders and have the children act out the conversations.

# 11  FEEDING THE FIVE THOUSAND

It is important for us to check our motivations when it comes to asking God to do things for us. Do we ask God for things in prayer because we want to be comfortable? Or do we ask because we truly want Him to be glorified? Explore this question with children as you discuss feeding the 5,000.

**Scripture Focus:** John 6:1-40

**Materials:**

- A roll or small loaf of bread (I used a bagel.)
- Two stuffed or plastic fish (If you really want a great WOW factor, use two sardines!)
- Poster of John 6:40

**Geography:** Sea of Galilee, Capernaum, Bethsaida

**Background:** Jesus left Cana and went back to Jerusalem for a feast. While there, Jesus went near the pool of Bethesda. Jesus walked by the pool and noticed a lame man. He had been lame for 38 years. Jesus told the man, *"Take up your bed and walk."* The man did just as Jesus said. After this the Jewish leaders persecuted Jesus and desired to kill Him because Jesus was doing these things on the Sabbath.

# OBJECT AND BIBLE LESSON

■ ■ ■ ■ ■ ■ ■ ■ ■ ■ ■ ■ ■ ■ ■ ■ ■ ■ ■ ■ ■

From Jerusalem, Jesus went back to the Sea of Galilee. In fact, He went across the Sea of Galilee. Jesus went up on the mountain and taught the disciples. A large crowd began to form because they had heard about the healings Jesus had performed. This area was deserted and remote.

Jesus asked Philip, *"Where can we get bread for these people?"*

**{Ask:}**

- Do you think Jesus already knew the answer to His question? [*Yes*]
- Why? [*Scripture says Jesus already knew His plan, but He wanted to test Philip.*]

Philip responded by saying even 200 denarii worth of bread would not be enough to feed them all. Andrew then told Jesus that there was a boy in the crowd who had five loaves of bread and two fish. Jesus told the disciples to seat the people.

Five thousand men sat down. That number does not include the number of women and children who were there to see Jesus.

**{Hold up the bread and fish. Ask:}**

- Do you think this bread would be enough to feed all of you until you were full? [*No*]
- What would I need to do to make sure we had enough food? [*Allow for answers. Children might say to break it into really tiny pieces, share the entire loaf, go to the store for more, etc.*]

Jesus took the lunch, gave thanks for it, and then distributed it to His disciples. The disciples then shared it with all of those who were seated.

**{Break the bread and give everyone a small piece (unless there is a gluten allergy!). Ask:}**

- Why can Jesus have enough bread for everyone and I cannot? [*He is God and the Creator.*]
- Did we have any bread left over? [*No, or not much*]

Only the Creator of the bread and fish could do such a thing! The people ate as much as they wanted of the bread and fish. Afterward, Jesus told the disciples to gather up the leftover bread. They filled up 12 baskets!!

The people were amazed and said that Jesus was the Prophet who is to come into the world! Jesus knew they were only interested in the signs and wonders that He did. He knew they wanted to grab Him and make Him king. Therefore, Jesus withdrew from the crowd.

**{Ask:}**

- How did Jesus know what the people wanted to do with Him? [*Jesus knows what people are thinking. He is God. He is omniscient, or all knowing.*]

That night the disciples got into a boat to go across the sea to Capernaum. The water was rough and the wind was strong. They were about three or four miles out from the shore when they saw Jesus walking toward them on the water. They were scared!! Jesus told them, "*Do not be afraid. It is I.*" They took Him into the boat, and immediately the boat was at the land where they wanted to go.

**{Ask:}**

- What would happen if we tried to walk on water? [*We would sink. Gravity pulls us down.*]
- Why could Jesus walk on the water? [*Jesus was with God when all things were created. Jesus, being God, created the water; therefore, He controls the laws of science. Jesus is all powerful, or omnipotent. He has power over nature.*]

The next day, the people went back to find Jesus, but He was not where He had been the day before. They got into boats and went across the sea to Capernaum to find Jesus. After they found Him, they asked when He had gone to Capernaum.

But Jesus knew their motivation. He told them, "*You aren't seeking Me. I fed you yesterday, so now you want food. Do not ask for food that does not last, but food that endures. I am the bread. Whoever comes to Me will never hunger or thirst.*"

# LIFE APPLICATION

■■■■■■■■■■■■■■■■■■■■■■

What strange words!

**{Ask:}**

- Do you remember what Jesus said to the woman at the well? [*I will give you Living Water.*]
- What happens if you do not drink water? [*You die.*]
- What happens if you do not eat food? [*You die.*]
- So food and water are pretty important. If Jesus IS the bread and GIVES the water...does that mean Jesus is important? [*Yes*]

I wonder if Jesus was sad for the people. They did not come to seek HIM. They followed Him because they wanted something from Him. They wanted to see signs and wonders, and be given food...like a magic show with popcorn! Jesus is not magic. He is God!

**{Ask:}**

- Why do you seek Jesus? [*Allow for answers.*]
- Why do you go to church? Do you go just to be with friends? Or do you go because your parents take you? [*Allow for answers.*]

Jesus knows your motivation. He knows everything. If you are only looking for miracles, or for God to get you out of a mess you created yourself, then Jesus knows you don't want **Him** because of Who He is.

Jesus loves you because He created you. He wants you to love Him because He created you. He wants a **relationship** with you based on love, not on what He can do for you.

Verse 40 tells us exactly why God sent Jesus to the earth.

**{Show the poster. Ask:}**

- What is Jesus' purpose? [*For people to see Him and believe in Him so they might have eternal life*]

# FEEDING THE FIVE THOUSAND

- Do you believe in Jesus? [*Allow for answers. Counsel children if needed.*]

**What can we learn from the feeding of the 5,000? Jesus has power over nature because He multiplied the food and He walked on water. Jesus is also all knowing because He knew what the people were thinking and how they were motivated.**

# COMMENT BOX

**THINK:** What went well as you taught this lesson? What can you do better?

_____
_____
_____
_____
_____
_____
_____
_____
_____

**TIP:** Be sure to teach that Jesus is omnipresent (ever present), omniscient (all knowing), omnipotent (all powerful), and immutable (never changing).

# 12 THE BEATITUDES

Should people live according to the righteousness of the Pharisees? How should a person who has a right relationship with God live? Jesus used the Sermon on the Mount to explain a standard of righteousness that was new. Use this lesson to show how Christians can live a righteous life.

**Scripture Focus:** Matthew 5:1-12

**Materials:**

- Glass jar
- Vegetable oil
- Food coloring
- Water
- Hamburger printable (See Resources Page.)
- Poster of Matthew 5:3

**Geography:** Sea of Galilee

**Background:** Jesus was still in the early years of His ministry. He fed the 5,000. He walked on water, and He healed great multitudes of people. More and more people were coming to see what He was about. His time still "had not come." Therefore, He continued to slip away when the religious leaders caused issues.

THE BEATITUDES

# OBJECT AND BIBLE LESSON

■■■■■■■■■■■■■■■■■■■■■

**{Fill the glass jar half full with oil. Fill it the rest of the way with water. Add 2-3 drops of food coloring into the jar. Shake the jar and then let it sit. I prepared this ahead of time, but you could do it with the kids. Ask:}**

- Where is the water? [*On the bottom of the jar*]
- Where is the oil? [*At the top*]

When Jesus saw the multitudes coming toward Him, He went up on a mountain. He sat down and began to teach the people. It was Jesus' job to tell the people about the Father and eternal life in Heaven. In the Sermon on the Mount, Jesus mentioned Heaven 21 times. He also talked about righteousness five times in this sermon. This suggests that this sermon focused on these two topics: Heaven and righteousness.

Jesus gave the people a list by which to live. We call this list the Beatitudes.

**{Ask:}**

- What happens if I shake the jar? [*Shake the jar. Allow for answers. The water and oil mix, but then separate again.*]

When people claim to have faith in Jesus, that means Jesus is in charge of their lives. When Jesus is in charge, and the Holy Spirit is working to change hearts, then people begin to act more and more like Jesus. In this sermon, Jesus wanted to tell the people how God's people should live and the types of attitudes they will display. A person cannot belong to God and live however he wants to.

Just like the oil and water are both IN the jar, Christians live IN the world. But over time, the water and oil separate. Over time, those who have faith in Jesus will look different, or separate from, those who do not have faith in Jesus. Let's see what Jesus said.

**{Build the Hamburger by writing the Beatitudes in the printable. Answers are written at the end of each section.}**

# THE BEATITUDES

I LOVE HAMBURGERS! The ones right off the grill smell good. They look good. A good hamburger can make me happy. However, after eating a good hamburger, I will eventually get hungry again. The happiness fades.

If we consistently fill ourselves up with the Bread of Life and Living Water (Jesus), then we will have a different attitude toward people. The joy God gives us does not fade. Jesus told those listening to Him that if they wanted to be a part of the Kingdom of God, then they had to be righteous—GOD'S way.

Each of the Beatitudes begins with *"Blessed are those who…"* That word *blessed* means the same as *happy* or *fortunate*. Jesus has told us how to be happy! This type of happy is not what you feel when you receive a birthday gift or see a best friend. Jesus is talking about eternal happiness and joy that comes from the Holy Spirit.

**Bottom of the Bun (Poor in Spirit)** – The bottom of the bun is a solid foundation for the rest of the burger. The same goes with the Beatitudes. The first Beatitude is foundational for all the rest.

When Adam and Eve were in the garden and they disobeyed God by eating the fruit from the tree of the knowledge of good and evil, something died within them. Their spirits became poor. They were separated from God by a sin nature. Every person born has a sin nature.

We are poor in spirit when we realize we are separated from God by our sin nature. We have no way to please God. Once we accept Jesus as our Savior through faith, then John 3:16 tells us we have everlasting life.

This Beatitude describes the attitude of a person realizing that they need Jesus. Once a person comes to Jesus through faith, then theirs is the Kingdom of Heaven.

Therefore, **Poor in spirit → Kingdom of Heaven.**

**Cheese (Mourn)** – Once we realize that we have sinned and will always sin, then we need to take it seriously. God surely does. Sin should not make us happy. When we ask God to forgive us and are really sorry we committed those sins, then we will be forgiven and comforted. God is the only One who can help us.

This Beatitude describes the attitude of a person who mourns and is sad about their sins. Jesus sent the Holy Spirit to guide and comfort those who believe.

Therefore, **Those who mourn → Shall be comforted.**

**Tomato (Meek)** – Being meek does not mean being weak. Being meek means being humble. A meek person understands that God is in charge, and they are not. Meek people focus on others and not themselves. Remember what happened to the earth when Adam and Eve disobeyed God? The ground was cursed. But the meek are able to enjoy the beauty of the earth around them because they are not focused upon themselves.

This Beatitude describes the attitude of a person who puts themselves last. Because humble people notice other people and the world around them, they are free to enjoy the earth.

Therefore, **The meek → Inherit the earth.**

**Meat (Hungering and Thirsting and Merciful)** – Remember that Jesus called Himself the Bread of Life and that He had Living Water? The more you read your Bible, memorize Scripture, pray, and worship Jesus, the more you will hunger and thirst for Him. The more you thirst and hunger, the more your life will be transformed to look like Jesus.

This Beatitude describes the attitude of a person who seeks first the Kingdom of God. God wants to be found; He wants to satisfy you.

Therefore, **Hunger and thirst after righteousness → Be filled (satisfied).**

The more we learn about Jesus, the more compassionate we become. We are quick to extend mercy, kindness, and second chances to those who do not deserve it. If you want to receive mercy, then be sure you give it out to others.

This Beatitude describes the attitude of a person who gives mercy to those who do not deserve it. Those who give mercy will receive mercy.

Therefore, **The merciful → Shall receive mercy.**

**Onion (Pure in Heart)** – As we learn more about Jesus, and as we partake of the Bread and Living Water, Jesus will begin to help us think differently and change our actions. God will cleanse our hearts. This is what the word *sanctification* means. It's allowing God to clean your heart, your motives, your thoughts, your actions, your words...everything. It is a slow process.

This Beatitude describes the attitude of a person who wants Jesus to clean his heart from sin. If we allow God to show us the sins we need to get rid of, then, through grace, we will see Him as He works on us.

Therefore, **The pure in heart → Shall see God.**

**Lettuce (Peacemakers) –** Being a peacemaker means you try to not cause arguments or fights, or be a part of trouble and unrest. You must make peace with God, and you must be at peace with other people. You make peace with God when you ask Him to forgive you of your sins. The same is true when dealing with others. If you mess up, own up to it. Ask for forgiveness. Make peace. You also need to forgive other people. You can also help others know how to be at peace with God and others.

This Beatitude describes the attitude of a person who desires to be at peace with God and with others. People who do this are called sons of God because they are righteous through Jesus.

Therefore, **The peacemakers → Called sons of God.**

**Top Bun (Persecuted) –** It does not sound quite right to say, "*Happy, or joyful, are those who are persecuted.*" Yet that is what Jesus was saying. Think about Jesus. The Jewish leaders tried to trick Him. They beat Him, pulled His beard, had Him whipped, nailed Him to a cross, and killed Him. Jesus had done nothing wrong. He did not feel "happy," but there is an unexplainable joy that comes from the Holy Spirit when you choose to walk in the ways of Jesus.

Jesus was persecuted, and He tells us over and over again in Scripture to be ready, for if we are going to follow Him, then we must carry our cross. We will be persecuted if we choose to be like Jesus.

**{Hold up the jar. The oil and water should be separated again.}**

If the water represents those who have faith in Jesus, and the oil equals those who do not believe, then we cannot mix. If we choose to be righteous like Jesus, then we will be radically different from the world. We will stand out. Nonbelievers do not understand Christians. They do not understand Jesus. They will not understand you either, if you have faith in Jesus.

This Beatitude describes the attitude of a person who is hurt because of his faith in Jesus. Sometimes this means the person dies. To be absent from the body is to be in the presence of Jesus. Where is Jesus? He's in Heaven. When you hurt because of your faith, remember that you will be in Heaven with Jesus one day.

Therefore, **Those who are persecuted for righteousness' sake → Theirs is the Kingdom of Heaven.**

**Toothpick (Rejoice)** – Some fancy sandwiches have toothpicks that keep them together. God gives our hamburger a toothpick. Jesus told the people to be happy if people persecuted them. Why? Because God has a reward waiting. We are to rejoice! If people think you are worth persecuting, then you must be acting like Jesus. We are to rejoice! Think of your favorite birthday gift. How much better will the gifts from God be? After all, He created things like stars, Saturn, and the ocean!!

Therefore, **when they persecute you, rejoice! Great is your reward in Heaven.**

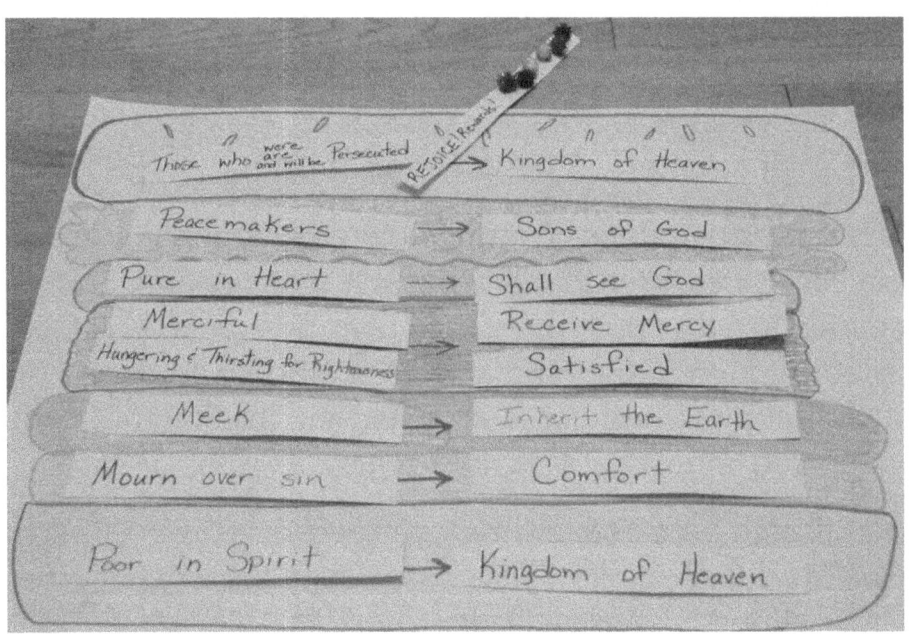

All of these "happys" and "blesseds" rest on the first one: *"Blessed are the poor in spirit."* Recognize that you are a sinner. Those who say they have no sin deceive themselves. Mourn over your sin. Allow God to work in you and transform you into a copy of His Son.

The Kingdom of Heaven is a place you do not want to miss. The only way you can be righteous is through faith in Jesus Christ.

**What can we learn from the Beatitudes? The Pharisees wanted to follow the law and be righteous and right with God. Jesus came to show us that it is faith in Him that makes us right with God. It is God who changes us into righteous people. We cannot change ourselves. God must be the One to do it.**

THE BEATITUDES

# COMMENT BOX

■ ■ ■ ■ ■ ■ ■ ■ ■ ■ ■ ■ ■ ■ ■ ■ ■ ■ ■ ■

**THINK:** What went well as you taught this lesson? What can you do better?

_____
_____
_____
_____
_____
_____
_____
_____
_____

**TIP:** The Beatitudes list is a great Scripture passage to have children memorize. Consider typing out the Scripture and awarding a prize to each child who memorizes all of it.

# 13  JESUS HEALS THE BLIND MAN

Who is Jesus? This is a very good question. Many in the world have the incorrect answer. Use play dough to teach children about Who Jesus is in this object lesson.

**Scripture Focus:** John 9

**Materials:**

- Play dough
- Two different play dough molds
- Poster of John 9:5

**Geography:** Jerusalem

**Background:** More and more people were following Jesus and bringing the sick and diseased for Him to heal. The words that Jesus taught showed an authority that baffled many, and they wondered if He could be the Christ. The Jewish leaders continued to watch Jesus. They engaged in conversations where they might trap Him saying something wrong. Nicodemus, the one who had come to Jesus at night, argued for Jesus and against the Pharisees at one point. The Bible tells us that Nicodemus became *"one of them,"* which means he became a follower of Jesus.

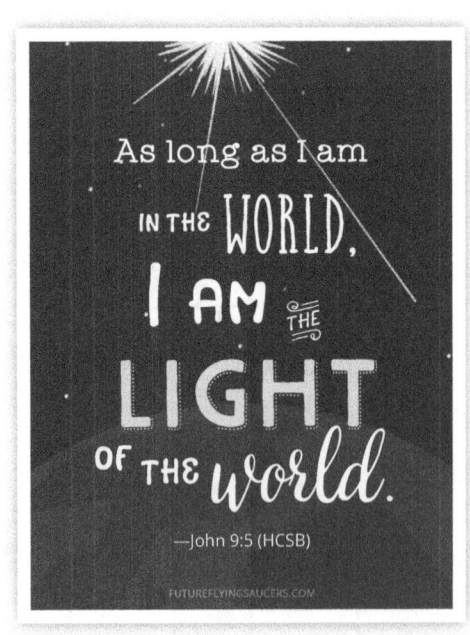

# OBJECT LESSON

**{Hold up the play dough and one of the molds. Have a conversation while you make the mold impression. Ask:}**

- What happens if I push the dough into the mold? [*It becomes the shape of the mold.*]

- Can I make more than one shape? [*Yes, I can use more play dough to make another shape.*]

- Can I put the molded play dough back into the mold? Will it fit? [*Yes*]

- Will this molded play dough match this second mold? [*No*]

- What will happen if I try to put this molded play dough into a mold it does not fit into? [*Play dough will squirt out of the sides; the other molded shape will be ruined.*]

Let's pretend that we are the Pharisees and that we have an idea of Who we think God is. We have studied and studied the Scriptures. We want to please God in all things.

Let's say the play dough is Jesus. The Pharisees wanted Jesus, and the expected Messiah, to fit into their little mold. They wanted Him to do exactly what they thought He should do. The problem is that people are not in charge of this world. God is.

Over and over Jesus tried to explain to the Pharisees (and whoever else was listening) Who He was and Who sent Him. But that did not fit the mold of the Pharisees and the people. The Pharisees became upset when Jesus did not do what they thought He should do. When Jesus healed a blind man on the Sabbath, it caused a problem.

JESUS HEALS THE BLIND MAN

# BIBLE LESSON

Jesus and the disciples passed by a blind man who was begging for money. The disciples asked Jesus, *"Who sinned? The man, or his parents?"* They thought bad things happened to people because of sins they committed.

**{Ask:}**

- Why do bad things happen in this world? [*Bad things happen because we live in a fallen world, an imperfect world. People are sinful and make poor choices.*]

Sometimes we perform actions or have behaviors that make bad things happen, because all actions have consequences. When bad things happen for no apparent reason, we must remember that we live in a world that is fallen.

Jesus explained to the disciples that the man was not blind because of sins committed by himself or his parents. The man was blind so God could glorify Himself. That was the reason why God allowed this man to be blind since birth. Jesus spat on the ground. He made some mud or clay {**hold up the play dough**} and placed it on the man's eyes. Jesus told the man to go wash in the pool of Siloam. The man washed and then came back seeing! God was glorified!

The man's neighbors and those who had seen him blind started questioning what happened. *"Surely this isn't the same man?"* they asked. *"This must be someone else."* They couldn't believe that such a miracle could happen. They would not listen to the man's testimony.

The people took the man before the Pharisees. It did not help Jesus at all that He had made clay to heal a man on the Sabbath Day. It was against the traditions of the Rabbis to knead clay on the Sabbath. The Pharisees asked the man what had happened. He told his story once again.

The Pharisees claimed that Jesus was not a man of God because He had not kept the Sabbath the way they thought it should be kept.

**{Hold up the different mold and the molded play dough. Try to fit them together. The first molded shape will become ruined.}**

Jesus was not fitting into their mold. The Pharisees called the parents of the blind man before them to see if this man truly had been blind since birth. The parents were intimidated because the Pharisees were going to "put out" of the synagogue (not allow to worship there any more) anyone who claimed Jesus as the Christ.

The parents told the Pharisees to talk to their son because he was old enough to answer for himself. Again the man was brought before the Pharisees. He told his story again. "*One thing I know,*" the man said, "*I once was blind, but now I see!*" After more arguing, the Pharisees cast him out of the synagogue.

**Then Jesus found him.** Jesus asked the man, "*Do you believe in the Son of Man?*" The man who was once blind replied that he did believe, and he worshiped Jesus.

# LIFE APPLICATION

■ ■ ■ ■ ■ ■ ■ ■ ■ ■ ■ ■ ■ ■ ■ ■ ■ ■ ■ ■ ■ ■ ■

It is so great to know that Jesus will find us when we have been cast away. That man had been telling the truth. Since what happened did not fit into the mold of the Pharisees, they cast him away.

People cannot argue away your personal relationship and experiences with Jesus. They cannot refute it. They can cast you away, ignore you, mock you, and hurt you. They cannot change the truth that Jesus does things that are unexplained and unexpected in your life.

Sometimes when we have a need and we go to Jesus with it, we expect Him to answer our prayer exactly how WE want it to be answered.

**{Hold up the mold.}**

We try to fit Jesus into our mold. Some people call this "putting God into a box." Scripture tells us that God wants to do immeasurably more than (literally means "more than more than"!) anything we can imagine (Ephesians 3:20). He wants to do "more than more than" we can imagine in our lives. Waiting and watching God do "more than more than" can be amazing!!

The blind man had no problem accepting Jesus for Who He was. He was not even sure WHO Jesus was, but he knew that he had once been blind…and NOW, after Jesus, he could see.

Some of the Pharisees never understood that. They never would see Jesus as being the Messiah because He did not fit into their idea of who the Messiah ought to be.

And the good news is: the early church was filed with believing Pharisees and other religious leaders who did accept Jesus as the Messiah. One of them you have already learned about.

If you have encountered Jesus—if you believe in the Son of Man—then you have a testimony like the blind man. Go and tell your story of Jesus to someone!

**What can we learn from Jesus healing the blind man?** ***"Do you believe in the Son of Man?"*** **Do you have your own idea of who God is? Be sure it matches**

what the Bible says. There will be times when bad things happen, or God does not answer prayer requests the way we want Him to. That is when we try to fit God into our own mold, or our own idea of Who He is. If you really believe in the Son of Man, Jesus, then understand that He is in charge, not you.

JESUS HEALS THE BLIND MAN

# COMMENT BOX

██████████████████████

**THINK:** What went well as you taught this lesson? What can you do better?

_____
_____
_____
_____
_____
_____
_____
_____
_____
_____

**TIP:** When I squashed the molded dough into the second mold, the children reacted strongly because I "ruined" the shape I had. Use reactions like this to your advantage when teaching children.

# 14 THE KINGDOM OF HEAVEN

During the beginning of Jesus' ministry, He performed many miracles. In the gospel of Matthew, after the Jewish leaders began to reject Him, Jesus started teaching in parables. This lesson focuses on some of Jesus' parables about the Kingdom of Heaven, as well as what those parables mean for us today.

**Scripture Focus:** Matthew 13:31-34, 44-46

**Materials:**

- 1/3 cup hydrogen peroxide (I used a 12% solution for a greater effect.)
- 8-10 drops of liquid dish soap
- 2 packages of dry yeast
- Large glass bowl
- Drinking glass
- Food coloring
- Smaller drinking glass
- Spoon
- 1/3 cup of hot tap water
- Poster of Matthew 13:44

**{This science experiment is a chemical reaction. You will want to do this with ventilation. It also puts off heat—enough to feel, but not to hurt. You can prepare the experiment with the children or ahead of time.}**

**Geography:** A town near the Sea of Galilee, possibly Capernaum

**Background:** The scribes and Pharisees were not accepting Jesus as the Messiah. In fact, they were accusing Him of working miracles using the power of Satan. Because of the challenges of the Jewish leaders and the fact that they wanted signs before they would believe Jesus was the Messiah, Jesus began to teach His disciples using parables.

The disciples noticed this change in Jesus' teaching. In Matthew 13:10, the disciples asked why Jesus was using parables. The word *parable* means "to come alongside" or "to throw alongside." Jesus began to teach using stories that compared something known to something that is unknown.

# OBJECT LESSON

■ ■ ■ ■ ■ ■ ■ ■ ■ ■ ■ ■ ■ ■ ■ ■ ■ ■ ■ ■ ■ ■

**{Put the large glass bowl on the table. Place the drinking glass in the center of the bowl. Pour the hydrogen peroxide into the drinking glass; add the dish soap and a few drops of food coloring. Mix carefully by swishing the glass around. In the other glass, pour in the hot tap water. Add the packages of dry yeast to the water. Mix well with the spoon. Ask:}**

- What makes most bread soft and fluffy? [*Allow for answers. The yeast reacts to the liquid and heat in the bread dough, causing the dough to rise slowly.*]

- What would happen to bread if we did not use yeast? [*It would be flat like pita bread or crackers.*]

- How would you describe the glass of yeast and water? [*Allow for answers. The children may describe it as brown, yucky, smells, gloppy, etc.*]

In our experiment, the yeast in the water is going to be a *catalyst*, or something that causes something else to happen.

**{Pour the yeast mixture into the hydrogen peroxide mixture. All of the foam should stay in the bowl, but it is fun to watch! If you have a smaller group of children, you can let them put their fingers in the foam and then wash hands.}**

The yeast did not look like much when it was in the small glass, but once it mixed with the liquid in the other glass, WOW! It expanded fast!!

THE KINGDOM OF HEAVEN

# BIBLE LESSON

**{Read Matthew 13:31-33.}**

We are going to learn about four parables that Jesus taught. Jesus described the Kingdom of Heaven through parables. This meant that He compared the Kingdom of Heaven with everyday items or everyday events.

In the first parable, Jesus compared the Kingdom of Heaven to a mustard seed. A mustard seed in Bible times was the smallest seed planted in an orchard. A mustard tree can grow to be about 12 to 15 feet tall. A large, healthy tree can grow from a small, insignificant seed.

Then Jesus compared the Kingdom of Heaven to leaven, or yeast. The woman put the leaven in the bread, or meal, until all of the dough was mixed well. When the bread rose and was baked, the yeast caused wonderful fluffy bread to be created.

Think about the yeast we used. It was small and brown, and it smelled bad. Once we mixed it with that other liquid, it expanded. It mixed with the food coloring and created beautiful foam.

Let us review what we know about the Kingdom of Heaven. We know that the Kingdom of Heaven is going to be like a small mustard seed. It will also be like yeast. Both start out small and insignificant; then they grow, or expand, into something beautiful, useful, and important.

**{Read Matthew 13:44-46. Ask:}**

- What did the man find in the field? [*A treasure*]

- What did he do with that treasure? [*He found it and then he hid it.*]

- What did the man do next? [*He sold everything he had and bought the field.*]

- What emotion did the man express when he did all of this? [*Joy*]

- Why do you think he felt joy? [*Allow for answers. What the man found in the field was better than everything he owned. Receiving that treasure brought him joy.*]

- For what was the merchant seeking? [*Beautiful pearls*]
- What did the man do when he found it? [*He sold everything he had and bought the pearl.*]
- According to this Scripture, what two things represent the Kingdom of Heaven? [*A found treasure in a field and an expensive pearl*]
- What were these two things worth to the men? [*They were worth everything.*]

Let us review again: We know that the Kingdom of Heaven is going to be like a small mustard seed. It will also be like yeast. Both start out small and insignificant and then grow into something beautiful, useful, and important.

We have also learned that the Kingdom of Heaven is a treasure that brings joy to the man who bought it. The Kingdom of Heaven was expensive and cost the merchant everything.

# LIFE APPLICATION

Keep in mind that parables are stories that are given alongside of a truth. Jesus wants to teach us something with these parables. He did not explain these four parables like He explained some of His other ones. We are not exactly sure what He meant by these parables, but we can get some good lessons from them.

**{Ask:}**

- What is the Kingdom of Heaven? [*Allow for answers. Lead children to think about a king and a kingdom. In other Scripture the term Kingdom of God is used; the Kingdom of Heaven = God's reign.*]

Jesus came to earth to redeem Israel and the Gentiles. He brought eternal life to all men. Those who believed in Him would start out as a small group of disciples; eventually that group would grow and be significant.

Those who have faith in Christ Jesus join God's family where God reigns supreme. God's Kingdom reigns now and will reign when Jesus returns. That is one reason why Jesus taught us to pray, *"Your kingdom come. Your will be done on earth as it is in heaven."*

When you are a part of God's Kingdom, it becomes so precious to you that you are willing to give up everything for it—and not only to give up everything, but to give it all up with an attitude of joy. In other words, if God asked you to do something, such as give all your Legos away to someone who had none, would you do it?

**{Ask:}**

- If you believe in Jesus, how much do you treasure Him? [*Allow for answers.*]
- Why should you treasure Jesus? [*Allow for answers. Jesus took all of God's wrath upon Him when He died on the cross, instead of allowing God's wrath to be on you. The wages of sin is death, but God chose to have Jesus die for you. Jesus died and rose again and now sits on the throne. If you have faith in Jesus, then He is your King. He is the treasure.*]
- Why should you be willing to give up everything for God's Kingdom? [*Jesus, like the merchant who bought the pearl, sacrificed everything so that He could*

*purchase you back from sin. He gave up everything for you; you should be willing to serve Him and allow Him to be your King and Master.*]

Your heart is a throne. Who sits on your throne? You? Or Jesus? Whoever sits on the throne is in charge of your life.

**What can we learn from the Kingdom of Heaven parables? God reigns over His Kingdom. Jesus is His Son. We can be a part of God's Kingdom, but that means He must be our King and Master. Because God loved us, Jesus died so that we could be in the Kingdom through faith in Him.**

THE KINGDOM OF HEAVEN

# COMMENT BOX

▮▮▮▮▮▮▮▮▮▮▮▮▮▮▮▮▮▮▮▮

**THINK:** What went well as you taught this lesson? What can you do better?

_____
_____
_____
_____
_____
_____
_____
_____
_____

**TIP:** For a different foam effect, you could use a soda bottle instead of a drinking glass in the large bowl.

# 15 JESUS IS THE GOOD SHEPHERD

Jesus called Himself a Shepherd. What does that mean and is it significant? This lesson will help children understand that people need a Savior and a Leader, and that we cannot live our lives in our own power.

**Scripture Focus:** John 10:1-16

**Materials:**

- Clip art pictures of a sheep pen, a shepherd, and a thief (See Resource Page.)
- Poster of John 10:9

**Geography:** Jerusalem

**Background:** Jesus healed the blind man and caused upheaval among the Jewish leadership. As more and more people began to follow Jesus, the Pharisees wanted more and more to get rid of Him.

# BIBLE LESSON

**{Ask:}**

- What do you know about being a shepherd? [*Allow for answers.*]
- Why do sheep need a shepherd? [*Allow for answers.*]

Shepherds during Bible times possibly kept a breed of sheep called fat-tailed sheep (Ex. 29:22; Lev. 3:9). This breed has a tail that stores fat, like a camel stores fat in a hump.

Sheep can have a number of problems. They can get over-heated in too much sun. They can get scratched by thorns. They need help crossing streams and finding good food. If sheep stray, they can become utterly helpless. Sheep can become scattered as well. Sheep were important because they were used for their meat, wool, and milk. They were also used as sacrifices in the temple.

**{Create a chart with three columns. Label one "The Good Shepherd," another "The Thief," and the third "The Hired Hand." Put the clip art images at the top of each column. As you read through the Scripture, you will add information to the appropriate columns as you learn about each person. Read John 10:1-16.}**

# JESUS IS THE GOOD SHEPHERD

| The Good Shepherd | The Thief/Stranger/Wolf | The Hired Hand |
|---|---|---|
| Enters by the door<br>Gatekeeper lets Him in<br>Sheep hear His voice<br>Calls sheep by name and leads them out<br>Goes before the sheep<br>The sheep follow Him<br>Gives life abundantly<br>Lays down His life for the sheep<br>Knows His own and they know Him | Does not enter by the door<br>Climbs in another way<br>Sheep will not follow<br>Sheep flee from him<br>The sheep do not know his voice<br>Came before Jesus<br>The sheep do not hear<br>Steals, kills, and destroys<br>Snatches and scatters the sheep | Does not own the sheep<br>When in danger, leaves the sheep and flees<br>Not concerned about the sheep |

**{Review the chart by holding up the individual pictures and discussing what the chart says about each.}**

Keep in mind that Jesus was speaking to the Jews. They would have been familiar with the life of a shepherd because many sheep were brought to the temple for sacrifices. Jesus used everyday life to teach heavenly concepts.

Most shepherds were outcasts. They did not necessarily take care of their own sheep, but rather sheep that belonged to their master.

Sheep are not smart animals. If you look at our sinful track records, we people really are not smart at times either. We make bad decisions that could hurt us or others. We are sinful, broken sheep.

In verse 16, Jesus told the Jews that He had sheep of another fold and that He was going to join both groups into one flock—one flock with one Shepherd.

# LIFE APPLICATION

**{Hold up, or point to, the clip art pictures. Ask:}**

- Who are the sheep? [*People*]
- Who is the Good Shepherd? [*Jesus*]
- Is the Good Shepherd the shepherd of all the sheep? [*No, He is only the shepherd of the ones who hear His voice and follow.*]
- Who is the thief or the wolf? [*Satan*]
- Who is the hired hand? [*Religious leaders*]

Christians follow the Good Shepherd. We need to watch out for the thief. We cannot rely on the hired hand. Jesus is the only One who willingly gives His life for you.

If you have faith in Jesus, then you listen to His voice that is good and true. You need to watch out for thoughts that lead to temptation and sin. Do not blindly take the word of church leaders, even me. Check what I say. Read the Bible for yourself.

Satan would love to destroy you. There will always be people who have their own selfish motives and reasons for not taking care of the sheep. You must ALWAYS listen to Jesus and know Him so that you hear His voice above all the noise.

Verse 14 is so important! Jesus KNOWS who belongs to Him.

Do you belong to Jesus? Would He say that you belong to Him? Do you listen to His voice? He laid down His life for you.

**{Ask:}**

- When did He do that? [*On the cross*]

That is why He calls Himself the Door, or the Gate. Jesus is the way to salvation (a right relationship with God through faith). All sheep must pass through the Door to enter into Heaven.

# JESUS IS THE GOOD SHEPHERD

Jesus is the only way. There is one flock and one Shepherd. Are you a part of His flock?

**What can we learn from Jesus' being the Good Shephard? Just as a shepherd leads, guides, and cares for sheep, Jesus wants to lead, guide, and care for you. Jesus laid down His life for you. He is the Door who leads to God.**

# COMMENT BOX

**THINK:** What went well as you taught this lesson? What can you do better?

_____
_____
_____
_____
_____
_____
_____
_____
_____

**TIP:** Always be prepared to counsel a child to choose Jesus. See the Extra Resources section of this book for how to do this.

# 16 THE PASSOVER

What does the Passover have to do with the church of today? And why does it matter? Create the Seder meal and bring the story of Passover, Jesus, and the Last Supper to life.

**Scripture Focus**: Matthew 26:26-30; John 13:3-15

**Materials:**

- Plate
- Wooden spoon
- Large bowl of water
- Candle
- 4 nice cups
- Napkin
- Matzo
- Small bowl of salt water
- Parsley
- Boiled egg
- Horseradish
- Lamb bone

- Charoset (For recipe: https://www.allrecipes.com/recipe/217287/passover-apples-and-honey-charoset)

- THIS WEBSITE (https://www.chosenpeople.com/site/sharing-the-gospel-through-the-passover-seder/) has a fantastic explanation of each part of the feast and what it represents, and how Jesus is reflected in the Passover. PLEASE read it! I will not repeat the information they have there, but incorporate it into the Bible event and show the objects.

I did this as an example for you. So you should do as I have done for you.

—John 13:15 (ICB)

THE PASSOVER

**Geography:** Jerusalem

**Background:** Do you remember what Jesus told His mother at the wedding in Cana? He told her that His time had not yet come. At this point in His life, Jesus knew His time had come. After the Triumphal Entry into Jerusalem, the Pharisees were ready to see Jesus die, and they received help from Judas Iscariot. Jerusalem swarmed with people as the Passover feast began.

THE PASSOVER

# OBJECT LESSON

**{You will use all of the props to show each step of the Passover meal. You might want to have everything arranged on a table as you do the lesson. Pick up the wooden spoon.}**

The disciples found an upper room in a house for them to celebrate their Passover feast together. Jews celebrating Passover would cleanse the room of all leaven. Sometimes parents would hide a few pieces of bread and the children would search for the bread. When it was found, they would take a feather and sweep the bread onto the wooden spoon to rid the house of the leaven.

**{Washing the feet – pick up the bowl.}**

Jesus took a bowl and took off His tunic. He began to wash the disciples' feet. When He got to Peter, Peter refused to have Jesus wash him. Jesus explained that Peter could have no part of Him if He did not. Then Peter responded, *"Not just my feet, but my hands and head, too!"*

**{Ask:}**

- Do you think Jesus washed Judas Iscariot's feet? [*Allow for answers. Yes, Jesus did wash Judas' feet.*]
- What do you think Jesus might have been thinking or feeling as He washed Judas' feet? [*Allow for answers. Jesus probably felt sad, but He was focused on why Judas was about to betray Him. Help children to understand that Jesus knew He was to die for the sins of all humanity...that means the sins of Judas AND each person, including each child.*]

**{Lighting the candles – light the candle.}**

During the Seder meal, after the washing of the feet, Jesus and the disciples would have lit the candles. Jesus had stated in the past that He was the Light of the World.

Then Jesus and the disciples would have told the Exodus story.

**{Have the students tell the highlights of the Exodus story including Moses, Pharaoh, the plagues, and the Passover.}**

# THE PASSOVER

Exodus tells of **Redemption**:

1. The slaves were in bondage.

2. God, through Moses, redeemed the Israelites. Being REDEEMED means being saved. God saved the Israelites from slavery.

3. Being redeemed costs something. It isn't free. Many sheep died so their blood could be put across the wooden door frames.

4. The blood brought FREEDOM to the Israelites.

Jesus and His disciples would have then passed the first cup of wine: The Cup of Blessings.

**{Show the first cup.}**

Then the second cup: The Cup of Plagues.

**{Show the second cup.}**

Jesus and the disciples would have done a curious tradition next. There would have been a bag on the table with three pieces of bread in it.

**{Take out 3 pieces of matzo bread. Place them on top of each other.}**

The bottom piece represented the Jews, or God's people. The top piece represented God. The middle piece represented the high priest. At this point of the meal, Jesus would have taken the middle piece and broken it in half. Half would go back into the bag with the other pieces; the other half would be wrapped in a napkin and hidden in the room.

**{Break the middle piece and wrap half in the napkin. Have a child "hide" the piece of bread.}**

Next is the Seder plate.

**{Have the parsley, small bowl of water, egg, horseradish, charoset, and lamb bone on the plate.}**

# THE PASSOVER

At this point, Jesus and the disciples would have eaten a meal together. It was during this time that Jesus told the group of disciples that one of them would betray Him.

They each asked, "*Is it I?*" They even asked John, who was sitting next to Jesus, to ask Him who would be the betrayer. Jesus responded, "*He who dips his bread with Me.*" Judas then asked, "*Is it me?*" And Jesus told him to go do what he needed to do quickly. So Judas left the group.

Then the hunt to find the hidden bread took place.

**{Have the child retrieve the hidden bread. Or, if you have a small group, allow the kids to hunt for it!}**

Once the bread was found, this possibly could have been the bread that Jesus then broke. Remember, this was the middle piece of bread representing the high priest, the mediator between God and man.

The book of Hebrews describes Jesus as our High Priest.

Jesus took the bread, broke it, and said, "*Take. Eat. This is my body.*" This portion of the bread had been hidden, just as Jesus' body would be hidden in the ground for three days. Then the bread was found, just as His body was raised to life.

Then Jesus probably picked up the third cup of the meal: the Cup of Redemption. He said, "*Take. Drink. This is my blood of the new covenant.*"

The New Covenant tells us about **Redemption**:

# THE PASSOVER

1. Like the slaves were in bondage in Egypt, we are in bondage to SIN.

2. Through Moses, God REDEEMED the Israelites. Through JESUS, God redeemed us.

3. Being redeemed is not free. Many lambs died to free the Israelites. JESUS died on a wooden cross for us.

4. The blood of the lambs saved the Israelites from death. The blood of JESUS saves us from death, and faith in Him brings ETERNAL LIFE.

The fourth cup may not have been drunk by Jesus. He stated after the third cup that He would not drink of the fruit of the vine again until He was in His Father's Kingdom. This cup is called the Cup of Hallel, which means "Cup of Praise."

Jesus may not have drunk from the cup, but He did offer a prayer of praise called The Priestly Prayer in John 17. In this prayer He prayed for the disciples and also prayed for us.

He knew His time had come...and He was thinking about you.

# LIFE APPLICATION

**{Ask:}**

- Do you think Jesus took the Cup of Redemption seriously? [*Yes*]
- Should we? [*Yes*]
- What can we do during communion to take the bread and cup seriously? [*Allow for answers. Explain that we should pray, ask for forgiveness, forgive others, and be as specific about our sins as we can. This is a good time to discuss how your local church celebrates communion.*]

When we take communion, we need to really think about what that juice or wine stands for. That is expensive juice. It bought you. That blood freed you from sin. That blood spilled so yours does not have to.

**What can we learn from Jesus and the Passover? In the book of Genesis, God makes it clear that someone was going to defeat the serpent from the garden. In the book of Exodus, God makes it clear that it is the blood of the lamb that saved the people from death. Jesus made it clear that it is His body and blood that was broken for you that saves you from your sins.**

# COMMENT BOX

**THINK:** What went well as you taught this lesson? What can you do better?

_____
_____
_____
_____
_____
_____
_____
_____
_____

**TIP:** This lesson requires more preparation than the others, but it is worth the effort!

# 17 THE PASSION OF JESUS

What would it have been like to stand on Calvary Hill that afternoon? Use this Bible lesson to discuss the events and people of the crucifixion.

**Scripture Focus:** Luke 23:26, 32-56; John 19:17-42

**Materials:**

- A rough log or firewood
- 3 long nails
- Hammer
- Poster of Mark 15:37

**Geography:** Jerusalem

**Background:** The ministry of Jesus is at an end. After three years of Jesus' traveling, preaching, teaching, healing, and casting out demons, the Jewish leaders arrested Jesus through the help of Judas, one of Jesus' own disciples. After a trial and beatings, Jesus carried His own cross as far as He could. His blood flowed down His body and into the sand as He struggled up the hill called Calvary. Can you picture it?

Then Jesus cried in a loud voice and died.

—Mark 15:37 (ICB)

# OBJECT AND BIBLE LESSON

**{Show the log and ask:}**

- What is this? [*A piece of wood*]

**{Choose a volunteer and carefully have them hold it. We do not want splinters! Ask:}**

- How would you describe this wood? [*Rough, heavy, dirty*]
- If you had to carry this a long distance, what do you think would happen? [*Arms would start hurting, skin would get scratched, might get splinters, back would start to hurt, body would become sweaty*]

After seeing Pilate, Jesus was taken away to be crucified. He had been whipped and beaten. He had probably lost a lot of blood. When people lose blood, they become weak and their muscles do not work well.

This must have happened to Jesus because the soldiers had another man, named Simon of Cyrene, carry Jesus' cross the rest of the way to Calvary. This is an example of Jesus being fully human.

**{Ask:}**

- At any time could Jesus have said, "Nope. I'm not going to do this anymore. You may not hit me again." What made Him not do this? [*He loved us and chose to do what His Father wanted Him to do.*]
- Could Jesus have called angels to come let Him go? [*Yes*]
- Could Jesus have just vanished? [*Yes*]

**{Have the room be quiet. Begin to hammer the three nails into the wood. If your group is small enough, allow the kids to come one at a time to strike a nail with the hammer. Be sure to help the little children, and remind the older ones not hit too hard. If you have a large group, choose three or four children to use the hammer.}**

Jesus was God AND man. Jesus chose to place His God-ness to the side and be human. He could have stopped all of this at any time. He did not.

He chose to have nails driven through His hands and feet. He chose to allow sinful men to beat Him and spit in His face. Jesus chose to hang on the cross when He could have vanished at any time.

Two men were crucified on either side of Jesus. One of the men mocked and blasphemed (said mean words about) Jesus. The other man recognized Who Jesus was. We have no idea how this man knew Who Jesus was. Maybe Jesus was so famous that even criminals knew about Him.

The Jewish people keep time slightly differently than we do. They begin their 24 hours at 6:00 AM. In this Scripture, the sixth hour would have been 12:00 noon. There was darkness from the sixth hour until the ninth hour, which would have been 3:00 PM.

**{Ask:}**

- We do not know how dark it was, but what would you think if the sky went dark when you were eating your lunch and did not become light again until the afternoon? [*Allow for answers.*]
- What if the sun went dark? [*Allow for answers.*]

Around 3:00 in the afternoon it was still dark, and the veil in the temple was torn into two pieces. Jesus cried out, *"Into Your hands I place My Spirit."* Then He died.

A centurion, a Roman leader of 100 men, was watching all of this. He began to glorify God and exclaimed, *"Surely this was a righteous man!"*

The crowd that had been gawking and sneering at Jesus watched what happened and then turned away, beating their chests. When people beat their chests like this, usually it is out of mourning.

**{Ask:}**

- What did Joseph of Arimathea and Nicodemus do? [*They took Jesus off the cross and placed Him in the tomb.*]
- Who were they? [*They were disciples of Jesus; both were Jewish leaders and believed in Jesus.*]

Both men were of the Jewish leadership. Scripture tells us that Joseph was a disciple of Jesus.

# THE PASSION OF JESUS

Both men knew the Jewish Law. It was the time of Passover. It was the Friday before the Sabbath...yet they touched a dead body. This would make them ceremonially unclean.

Perhaps they were willing to become unclean because they understood what had happened on the cross. Maybe they knew their sin was no longer on them, but on Jesus.

**They were touching the unclean body that made THEM clean.** They were not afraid to get their hands dirty and serve the needs of Jesus.

Jesus was the **Sacrifice**, the Lamb who took away the sins of the world. Jesus died for all, but it is only when we have faith in Him that we can become friends with God and deal with our sin nature.

# LIFE APPLICATION

■ ■ ■ ■ ■ ■ ■ ■ ■ ■ ■ ■ ■ ■ ■ ■ ■ ■ ■ ■ ■

The second criminal asked Jesus to remember him when Jesus entered His Kingdom. Jesus told the criminal he would be in Paradise with Him that day. This is an example of salvation through faith. That criminal could do nothing for Jesus. He couldn't be baptized. He couldn't do good works. All the man could do was surrender his heart and his will to Jesus through faith.

**{Show the wood with the nails.}**

You are a sinner. I am a sinner. We helped to hammer the nails into the wood of the cross. If we say we do not have sin, then we are lying to ourselves. God is holy. BUT! if you believe, in faith, that you are a sinner, and you submit to Jesus and allow Him to be your Master, then you have the gift of eternal life. Which criminal do you want to be like? They both were sinners, just like us. Yet one criminal believed in Jesus and the other did not.

**Once you choose to have a saving faith in Jesus, then your salvation is known BY your works.** The book of James tells us that faith without works is dead. Think of Joseph and Nicodemus. They acted on their faith.

Are we willing to get our hands dirty when serving others? Are we willing to step out from the angry crowd and tell others by our actions that we are disciples of Jesus?

Nicodemus carried 100 pounds of spices in order to prepare Jesus' body for burial. That was expensive and heavy. Are we willing to give up our money to help others? Are we willing to do hard work to help others?

**{Ask:}**

- List some ways that you can show your faith by your actions. [*Allow for answers such as obeying parents, using kind words, sitting with someone who is alone, doing work without complaining, etc.*]

**What can we learn from the Passion of Jesus? When Jesus, who was God, died on the cross, He revealed to people that He loved all of us. This is why His death is called the "Passion." He loved us enough to die a horrible death. He died so that we can have a complete relationship with God again. But He did not stay dead...**

# COMMENT BOX

**THINK:** What went well as you taught this lesson? What can you do better?

_____
_____
_____
_____
_____
_____
_____
_____
_____

**TIP:** See the FutureFlyingSaucers store for printable activities that go with the Last Supper, Good Friday, and Resurrection lessons.

# 18 THE RESURRECTION

Some people claim that Jesus did not die on the cross. Some people claim that Jesus was not resurrected. Some people claim that the disciples stole Jesus' body. What evidence do we have of the Resurrection of Jesus?

**Scripture Focus:** Matthew 27:62-28:11

**Materials:**

- Magnifying glass (even better if you have a detective's hat, too!)
- Poster of Matthew 28:6

**Background:** Jesus died on a cross. All of His disciples and followers deserted him, except some women and John, who would take care of Mary, Jesus' mother. Joseph of Arimathea and Nicodemus took the body of Jesus down from the cross, wrapped Him in linens, and laid Him in a tomb cut out of a rock.

THE RESURRECTION

# OBJECT AND BIBLE LESSON

■ ■ ■ ■ ■ ■ ■ ■ ■ ■ ■ ■ ■ ■ ■ ■ ■ ■ ■ ■ ■ ■

We are going to be Resurrection detectives today! What evidence do we have that Jesus actually rose from the grave?

**[Hold up the magnifying glass.]**

To answer our question, we need to search for clues. When solving a Biblical question, always look at Scripture first.

**{Read Matthew 27:62-28:11, then ask:}**

- What safety measures were in place to ensure that no one stole the body? [*The Jewish leaders had permission from Pilate to place a guard around the tomb. They also sealed the tomb.*]

- How many soldiers were placed at the tomb? [*Scripture does not say. In Matthew 28:11, it says that "some of the guard" went into the city. So that would mean that there were more than two or three guards. Pilate told the Jewish leaders to "make it as secure as you know how." There were at least 11 disciples. Therefore, there could have been at least 11 soldiers. This was also Passover weekend, so thousands of people would have been camped all over the mountain. These would have been people who shouted "Hosanna!" for Jesus a few days earlier. With all of this in mind, how many soldiers do YOU think would have been at the tomb?*]

- What sealed the tomb? [*A huge rock about four feet wide would have been used to seal the tomb. It would have been heavy for one person to move.*]

- What happened when Jesus was resurrected? [*There was an earthquake. An angel came down from Heaven, rolled back the stone, and sat on it. The guards were frightened.*]

- To whom did the angel speak? [*Mary Magdalene and the other Mary, who was the mother of James (Luke 24:10)*]

**{Look through the magnifying glass at the children, then ask:}**

History might change, but the way people act stays the same. People who lived during Bible times would have thought and felt just like you.

- Were there witnesses who saw the death of Jesus? [*Yes. Joseph of Arimathea, Nicodemus, Mary Magdalene, Mary the mother of James, possibly the apostle John, and Jesus' mother, Mary, witnessed Jesus' death. You can also include the Roman soldier who stated, "Surely this was the Son of God," when Jesus died.*]
- Were there witnesses who saw the body placed inside the tomb? [*Yes. Joseph, Nicodemus, Mary Magdalene, and Mary the mother of James saw Jesus' body placed in the tomb.*]
- When the women saw the angel, did they listen or ignore him? [*They listened and obeyed.*]
- Have you ever been really scared before? [*Allow for answers.*]
- After the situation was over, did you tell the story to someone? [*Allow for answers.*]
- Do you remember all the details? [*Allow for answers. Most will probably remember, because when we are scared our senses can be heightened.*]
- Can you think of other times in the Bible when angels appeared to people? [*Jacob, Daniel, Joshua, Isaiah, Ezekiel, Zechariah, Mary, the shepherds*]
- When they told people about their angel experience, do you think the people believed them? [*Yes*]
- Is there any reason why the experience for Mary Magdalene, the other Mary, and the soldiers would be any different? [*No*]
- Would they remember details? [*Yes*]

The people who went through the Resurrection experience were credible witnesses. The women told the disciples, and we know from other Scripture that Peter and John ran to the tomb to see for themselves.

**{Look through the magnifying glass and ask:}**

- If they had stolen the body of Jesus, do you think they would have run to the tomb? [*Probably not*]
- What might they have done differently? [*Allow for answers. If they stole the body, it makes sense that they would hide and leave town, if possible.*]

# BIBLE APPLICATION

You can continue studying Scripture to find even more evidence of the Resurrection. The important thing to remember is t think about what you read. The Bible is the true, inspired Word of God.

While God does not have to defend Himself, it IS good for YOU to know and understand what you believe about God.

What do YOU think after reading this Scripture and thinking about it? Did Jesus come back to life?

And if He did...what does that mean for you?

You have a Savior who lives. God is real. Because God exists, God is real, and God is alive, that means you need to deal with your sin.

The Bible says that all people are sinners and deserve death. We have a broken relationship with God. God is holy and merciful, and He sent Jesus to earth to die in our place. When you choose to believe in faith that Jesus came, died, and rose again, then you are adopted into God's family and you have eternal life.

**What can we learn from the Resurrection? God loved the world so much that He sent His only Son to die. He did not stay dead. Jesus is the Son of God and came back to life. The same power, God's power through the Holy Spirit, that raised Jesus from the dead is in you if you choose to let Jesus be your Master.**

THE RESURRECTION

# COMMENT BOX

■ ■ ■ ■ ■ ■ ■ ■ ■ ■ ■ ■ ■ ■ ■ ■ ■ ■ ■ ■ ■

**THINK:** What went well as you taught this lesson? What can you do better?

_____
_____
_____
_____
_____
_____
_____
_____
_____
_____

**TIP:** If you are using the color posters, be sure to review all of the main verses leading up to the Resurrection. Discuss how Jesus showed people that He was God.

# 19 THE ROAD TO EMMAUS

There is much about Jesus we do not understand. However, God has revealed SO much to us through the Scriptures. Use this Road to Emmaus object lesson to discuss Biblical revelation with children.

**Scripture Focus:** Luke 24:13-45; Deuteronomy 29:29

**Materials:**

- 3-4 copies of different children's mystery books
- Small mirror
- Poster of Luke 24:32

**Geography:** Jerusalem

**Background:** Jesus had died. He was placed in the tomb. The disciples were scared out of their wits and were hiding in a room somewhere. Sunday morning came, and the women reported that the stone was rolled away and that there was no body in the tomb. Peter and John ran to the tomb to see for themselves. Then all of the disciples locked themselves in the room. After all, would the Romans or Sanhedrin be after them next?

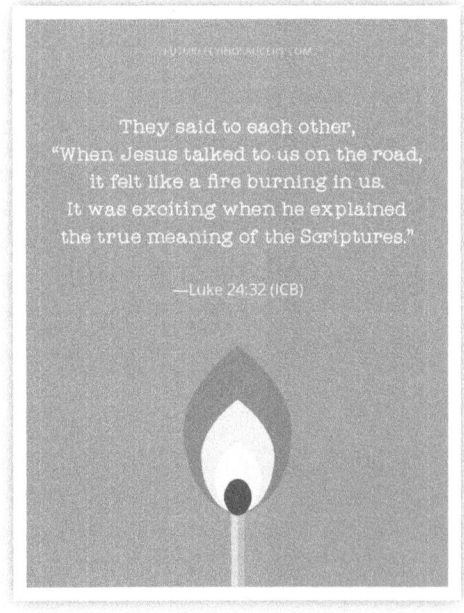

# OBJECT LESSON

**{Show the books and ask:}**

- Do you like mystery books? [*Allow for answers. Discuss favorite characters or story lines.*]

- What types of things make good mystery stories? [*Allow for answers. Discuss how authors weave clues throughout the story; sometimes you can figure out the puzzle and sometimes you cannot.*]

- Even though you might know something is a clue when you are reading the book, when do ALL of the clues make sense? [*At the end*]

We like to try to solve the mystery by the clues we read. It is always fun to see if we are right! In the end there is an "Ah-ha!" moment when everything makes sense.

God has a book for us to read called the Bible. Throughout it, He tells us clues about Who He is and about His plan. We need to study those clues so we can know more about the mystery of God.

THE ROAD TO EMMAUS

# BIBLE LESSON

**{Read Luke 24:13-45.}**

On the day that Jesus rose from the dead, He appeared to different people. Toward the end of the day, He appeared to two of His disciples who were walking from Jerusalem towards Emmaus, which was a 2-3 hour walk.

The Bible tells us that the eyes of the men were "restrained," or not allowed, to know that it was Jesus who joined them on their walk.

Jesus asked the men what they were talking about.

**{Ask:}**

- Because Jesus is God, do you think He already knew why the men were sad? [*Yes*]

- Why do you think He asked them about it then? [*Allow for answers. Perhaps it was a way to begin conversation. Recognizing the emotions of people around us is important; it allows us to talk to them about what they are feeling and could be a way to introduce Jesus to people.*]

The Bible says that one of the men was Cleopas. He seemed quite amazed that Jesus had not heard of what had happened over the last few days. The death and missing body of Jesus must have caused quite a stir.

**{Ask:}**

- Did Jesus really not know what had happened? [*No. He was Jesus. He was the One who had just died and risen again.*]

- Why do you think Jesus asked them about what happened? [*Allow for answers. It is possible that Jesus wanted them to go through all of the facts of the weekend BEFORE He took them on a journey through the Old Testament. He wanted them to voice some of the clues!*]

The two men told Jesus everything. Then Jesus started explaining to them all about the Old Testament prophets, including Moses. He also explained the Scriptures that were the clues about Himself, the Christ.

When they got to the village, the two men invited Jesus to stay with them. Jesus sat at the table to eat and broke the bread. At that moment, the Bible tells us that the eyes of the men "were opened" and they realized Jesus was with them.

**{Ask:}**

- After you read a good book or watch a great movie, what do you like to do? [*We like to talk about it and tell others to read or watch it.*]

That is what the men did! They started telling each other, *"Didn't our hearts burn inside when He was telling us about the Scriptures?"* Then they left in a hurry to go back to Jerusalem to tell the others.

The clues were revealed. These two men knew and understood Who was with them. Once they were with the others they said, *"The Lord has risen indeed, and has appeared to Simon!"*

**{Ask:}**

- Why were there only 11 disciples? [*Judas had hanged himself after feeling sorrow when Jesus was arrested by the Sanhedrin. (Matthew 27:3-10)*]
- Whom were the two men referring to when they said "Simon"? [*They probably were referring to Simon Peter, but we are not sure.*]

While all of this was going on, Jesus appeared in the room with the disciples. They were terrified and thought that He was a ghost. Jesus asked for food and ate it. He told them to touch His hands.

He told the disciples that everything that had happened over the past few days took place to fulfill the prophecies of the Old Testament.

THEN, Jesus "opened" the eyes of all of them. This was their "Ah-ha" moment! Everything made sense!

He opened their eyes, but he opened their minds as well! They finally understood what Jesus wanted them to know. Jesus had not come into the world to save Israel from Rome. It was MUCH larger than that!

Jesus had come to save humanity from sin. Jesus had come to allow men to have a relationship with God again. Jesus had come to earth to take God's wrath for man. And now the disciples understood.

Do you understand? Jesus came that you might have eternal life.

# LIFE APPLICATION

**{Read Deuteronomy 29:29.}**

God has given us the Bible. The Old Testament is filled with clues about how God is going to bring humanity back to Himself.

In the New Testament we learn how God chooses to save all mankind. We also are given clues about Jesus coming back to earth. This has not happened yet.

When you read the Bible, sometimes it makes sense, and other times we need help understanding what we are reading. Listen to your parents or Bible teacher when they teach you about the things of God. When do you that, it is possible that God will reveal something to you. God wants everyone to know about Him, but He only reveals Himself a little bit at a time.

**{Breathe across the mirror causing it to fog. Ask:}**

- When you take a hot bath, what happens to the mirror? [*It gets foggy.*]

The things of God can be foggy. He can be mysterious.

- But what happens as the bathroom cools? [*The water eventually fades away.*]

**{Show the clear mirror.}**

As you learn more about God, read the Bible, go to church, and listen to good advice from those who love Jesus, your mirror becomes less foggy. However, while we are on earth, our mirror will never be totally clear. That will not happen until we are in the presence of Jesus. THEN we can ask Jesus any question we might have, and our mirror will be clear. We will understand all kinds of things that confused us here on earth.

Many times, people will read something in the Scriptures, but they don't understand it; then they discount the Bible altogether. That is not what we are to do. We are to ask God, seek His face, go to Him, and give Him our confusions and worries.

We also need to remember that God is faithful and trustworthy.

# THE ROAD TO EMMAUS

**What can we learn from the road to Emmaus? God is not out to trick us. He is on our side. Life may seem foggy and confusing at times, but He wants to reveal Himself to you. He has plenty of clues for you. Are you listening?**

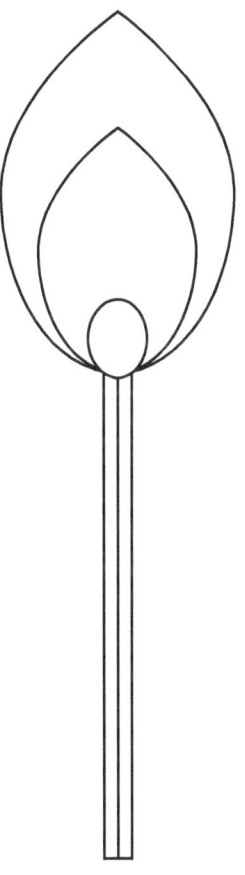

## COMMENT BOX

**THINK:** What went well as you taught this lesson? What can you do better?

_____
_____
_____
_____
_____
_____
_____
_____
_____

**TIP:** See the free Bible Reading Logs that are in the FutureFlyingSaucers store. Use these to help children begin the habit of reading the Bible on their own.

# 20 BREAD AND FISH BY THE SEA

When we have hard decisions to make or are in a stressful situation, Jesus wants us to talk to Him about it. In this lesson, focus on the fact that Jesus desires to spend time with His people. He cares about what we think and feel.

**Scripture Focus:** John 21:1-14

**Materials:**

- Fishing net (use the same one from The Twelve Disciples lesson)
- Bread roll
- Stuffed or plastic fish
- Poster of John 21:12

**Geography:** Sea of Galilee, also known as the Sea of Tiberias

**Background:** It happened so fast! Jesus was arrested, sentenced to death, and died on a cross within one day. Three days later, it was rumored that Jesus had risen from the dead! One by one, group by group, Jesus appeared to those who believed. He even appeared to some who doubted.

# OBJECT LESSON

**{Hold up the fishing net. Ask:}**

- Do you remember the lesson we talked about when we had this net? [*Allow for answers. Hopefully they will remember the lesson when Jesus called the 12 disciples.*]

- How many can use this net? [*A small group*]

- For what purpose is this net used? [*Catching fish*]

**{Put the net down and show the bread and fish. Review the lesson of Feeding the Five Thousand. Ask:}**

- What lesson can we learn from the feeding of the 5000? [*Allow for answers. Jesus had power over nature.*]

- What job did Peter, Andrew, James, and John have before they knew Jesus? [*They were fishermen.*]

# BIBLE LESSON

**{Read John 21:1-14. Ask:}**

- How many disciples went fishing? [*Seven*]

- Did they catch anything? [*No*]

- Why do you think they went fishing? [*They had been told to go to Galilee (Matthew 28:10) and that Jesus would see them there. Perhaps they chose to fish while they were waiting.*]

- Did the disciples know who was on the shore? [*No*]

- What directions were the disciples given? [*Jesus told the men to cast the net on the right side of the boat.*]

- What happened next? [*The net became full of large fish.*]

At this point, John, also known as the disciple whom Jesus loved, realized that it was Jesus who was calling out to them. John told Peter. Peter proceeded to put on his cloak and jump over the side of the boat, rushing to the shore.

The other disciples pulled the fish to shore in the boat.

When they reached the beach, the men saw that Jesus had a fire started and had been cooking fish. Jesus invited them to add more fish and to sit with Him and eat.

**{Show the fish and bread. Ask:}**

- Did all of the disciples know it was Jesus? [*Yes*]

- Why do you think Jesus wanted to eat with these men? [*Allow for answers. They were His friends. Eating together and fellowship is important. Perhaps He wanted to talk to them about everything that had happened after the Resurrection, and what would be happening in the future.*] During Jesus' crucifixion, all of the disciples had abandoned Him. The act of eating together was an ancient custom that was used to show forgiveness. Jesus had eaten with the disciples after the resurrection. Now He was doing it again to show the men that they were forgiven.

- What details are we told in this Scripture? [*Peter stopped to put on his outer garment; the boat was about 100 yards from land; Peter swam to shore, but then went back to drag the net to the beach; there were 153 large fish in the net; the net did not break.*]

That is a lot of details! The apostle John wrote this Scripture, and I wonder if he wanted to make sure that those who read his gospel had no doubts that he WAS there, and that he DID eat with Jesus.

# LIFE APPLICATION

We can also learn that when we obey the Lord Jesus, we will have great blessings. The men obeyed Jesus and cast their nets on the other side, and then they caught a huge amount of fish.

Remember when we talked about being fishers of men? If the church works together to tell people about Jesus, then they will be rewarded. The reward might not come here on earth, but they will be rewarded.

We can read in later verses that Jesus has a serious discussion with Simon Peter. Simon Peter had denied Jesus three times during the trial process before Jesus' death. Jesus wanted to restore this relationship with Peter because He had a special plan for Peter.

Jesus cared about His disciples. He knew that starting the church would be a hard task. He knew that they would need to be brave and bold. So He created a breakfast for them on the beach. Jesus wanted the disciples to have no doubts about the fact that they were forgiven and accepted by Him.

Something happens to relationships between people when they eat together.

**{Ask:}**

- Does your family sit together to eat meals? [*Allow for answers. Many children may say they do not. Explain that there are wonderful blessings that come with eating as a family together.*]
- If your family does not eat together, how do you eat your meals? [*Allow for answers.*]

When Jesus fed the 5,000, He had the people sit in groups. When He ate with the disciples, they sat around a campfire.

Jesus wants us to be in community with Him and with other people. Jesus knew that the disciples would need each other because He was about to leave them.

People need each other. Make sure you have friends who have faith in Jesus. If your family does not regularly eat together, talk to your mom or dad and see if you can do that more often. Eat together and have meaningful conversations.

Jesus did not sit with the disciples and watch television or play on His phone. No, He spoke with them. He taught them. He prayed with them. He encouraged them.

Television and computer games are not bad in and of themselves. However, if they distract you from being in fellowship and community with other people, then maybe you need to think about your actions.

**What can we learn from the bread and fish by the sea? Jesus loves you and He wants to spend time with you. He wants to hear about what you love and what hurts your heart. He wants to help you make decisions. He wants to encourage you. But you have to choose to spend time with Jesus.**

Jesus said to them,

"Come and eat."

None of the followers dared ask him,

"Who are you?"

They knew it was the Lord.

—John 21:12 (ICB)

## COMMENT BOX

■ ■ ■ ■ ■ ■ ■ ■ ■ ■ ■ ■ ■ ■ ■ ■ ■ ■ ■ ■

**THINK:** What went well as you taught this lesson? What can you do better?

_____
_____
_____
_____
_____
_____
_____
_____
_____

**TIP:** This is a culmination lesson which builds upon knowledge of previous lessons. Make sure to teach The Twelve Disciples and Feeding the Five Thousand first.

# BONUS: MAKE DISCIPLES OF THE NATIONS

When Jesus left the earth, He gave directions to the disciples. Those directions were not just for them. They are for ALL of those who choose to follow Jesus. Use this object lesson to teach children about taking the gospel to the nations.

**Scripture Focus:** Matthew 28:16-20; Acts 1:8-9

**Materials:**

- One small candy bar (or type of candy) for each child
- Bag or bowl that is not see-through
- Poster of Acts 1:8

**Geography:** Mountain in Galilee

**Background:** One by one, group by group, Jesus appeared to those who believed and even to some who still doubted. Jesus had appeared to the 11 disciples at least three times over the course of 40 days after His resurrection. It was now time for Jesus to return to His Father in Heaven.

# OBJECT LESSON

**{Put the candy bars in a bag or bowl. Choose one child to come to you, and whisper something like this: *"I have free candy bars! You may have one, but you now need to go tell one other person about the free candy bars!"* As each child comes up, tell them the same thing. If you have a large group, have the kids tell two others about the free candy. Watch the candy spread! Toward the end when almost everyone has candy, have your "evangelist" stand and loudly proclaim, *"Is there anyone else who still needs a free candy bar?"*}**

Was it fun and exciting to receive the free candy? You didn't have to do anything to receive it. All you had to do was come to me and I gave you one.

Once you received your free gift, you then shared the good news of candy with someone else.

**{Take up the candy, or have them place it under their chair, or on the floor in front of them or no one will listen to you. Hand it back out at the end of the lesson. Ask:}**

- What would you think if the first person took the free candy and then didn't tell anyone? [*He would be selfish; that is not fair.*]

MAKE DISCIPLES OF THE NATIONS

# BIBLE LESSON

Jesus appeared to the disciples one last time. This time He had some important instructions for the disciples.

It is interesting to know about the location Jesus used for this event. He had the disciples gather in a certain place in Galilee. The area was called "Galilee of the Nations" (Isaiah 9:1). This was significant because of the command Jesus was about to give the disciples.

**{Read Matthew 28:18-20 and Acts 1:8-9. Ask:}**

- Why do you think Jesus told the disciples that all authority had been given to Him? [*Allow for answers. Perhaps Jesus said this so the disciples would understand that His instructions were coming from God. Jesus was the Person to listen to and obey.*]

- What were the instructions? [They were to

    1. Go;
    2. Make disciples of ALL nations (not just the Jews);
    3. Baptize the new disciples as followers of Jesus; and
    4. Teach the new disciples to follow Jesus' commands.]

- In Whose name were they to baptize? [*The name of the Father, the Son, and the Holy Spirit*]

- Who is the Holy Spirit? [*Allow for answers. Possible answers include the dove that came down at Jesus' baptism; the third person of God; the Holy Spirit that is here on earth as our helper.*]

- What was the Holy Spirit going to do? [*He was going to come upon them in power.*]

- How do you think the disciples felt? [*Allow for answers. They may have felt excited, nervous, scared, or not sure what to expect.*]

- What did Jesus call the disciples? [*His witnesses*]

- Why did Jesus call them that? [*These people had seen many of His miracles, listened to His teaching, seen Him heal, watched Him die, and then experienced His resurrection.*]

- To where were these people to travel? [*Jerusalem, Judea, Samaria, and to the ends of the earth*]
- What do you think the disciples felt as they saw Jesus rise into the air and disappear? [*Allow for answers.*]

# LIFE APPLICATION

■ ■ ■ ■ ■ ■ ■ ■ ■ ■ ■ ■ ■ ■ ■ ■ ■ ■ ■ ■ ■ ■

If you follow Jesus, then that means someone shared the Good News of Jesus with you. You may have been baptized, and now you listen and learn from Bible teaching.

Do you remember what Jesus told Nicodemus? He said that we are to be born of water and born of the Spirit.

Being born as a baby is being born of water. When you have faith in Jesus, you are born of the Spirit. You have the Spirit of God within you. You have the same Spirit inside of you that raised Jesus from the dead!

What power we possess!

So why is it that we have a hard time sharing the "candy bar," or the Good News of Jesus, with people? A candy bar is nothing compared to the location of an eternal soul. We will either be with God in Heaven or separated from God in hell. That seems too important to not tell people!

So how do you fish for more men? For one thing, do not do it alone. Be sure you are a part of a local church that is willing to help you learn how to tell other people about Jesus. Practice telling your Jesus story.

Pray. Ask Jesus to show you who to tell your Jesus story to. Ask Jesus to tell you which friend to invite to a church activity. Jesus wants to help you tell the Good News. He will give you the boldness to say or do whatever needs to be said or done.

Serve. What can you do to help others around you? Jesus has prepared you for good works, so do them.

Be willing to go wherever God asks you and do whatever He wants you to do. Obey. And Jesus will allow you to have some amazing fishers-of-men experiences!

**What can we learn from making disciples of the nations? Jesus commanded with authority for His disciples to go, make disciples of all nations, baptize them, and teach them His commands. We need to be willing to do the same thing.**

# COMMENT BOX

**THINK:** What went well as you taught this lesson? What can you do better?

_____
_____
_____
_____
_____
_____
_____
_____
_____

**TIP:** Be encouraged! Through the power of the Holy Spirit, go and preach the Good News to children!

# EXTRA RESOURCES

# HOW TO LEAD A CHILD TO CHRIST

After you teach a Bible lesson, there are times when it is necessary to ask the children if they want to receive the gift of salvation through Jesus. Always have those who want to make some sort of decision leave the larger group of kids. I do this by either having them stay behind while the others leave, or taking the small group into another room. I do this because it causes the child to physically make a decision: *"Do I stay? Or not?"* This also allows for fewer distractions. (Always be sure to have another adult nearby. That's a safety rule!)

Ask many questions; you want the children to think through what they are doing. These questions should not be answered by "Yes," "No," or "Jesus." Use lots of Scripture, because you want God's Word to be working.

There is no minimum age for salvation. Even three-year-olds can recognize they are sinners and be sorry for what they do. However, you do want to be sure that the child, no matter the age, understands this lifelong commitment.

Salvation is a big deal, and you don't want a child to make a decision that is not understood or taken seriously. If at any point you sense that there is confusion or uncertainty on the child's part, say, *"I can tell that God is working in your heart. I want you to keep listening and learning."* Then dismiss that child who is not ready.

Examples of Counseling Questions:

1. Why have you decided to talk with me?
2. Why do you need Jesus as your Savior?
3. What is sin?
4. What are some examples of sin?
5. Can you do anything to get rid of sin?
6. Read Romans 3:23.

7. Who is Jesus?

8. What did Jesus do for you?

9. Read 1 Corinthians 15:3-4.

10. Read John 3:16 or Acts 16:31.

11. Would you like to pray to God and receive Jesus now?

If the child understands the questions and is answering appropriately, describe salvation as a heart change—a choice to move away from sin and toward God. If the child is serious about dealing with sin and wanting to live for Jesus, explain that he or she needs to talk to God and that talking to God is called prayer.

At this point lead the child in prayer. Have the child copy what you say or tell the child what information should be included when asking God for salvation:

- Admit to God you are a sinner.
- Say that you are sorry for those sins. Ask for forgiveness.
- Tell Jesus you believe Jesus is God's Son and that He died on the cross and rose again.
- Confess that Jesus is your Lord and Master.
- Thank God for saving you.

Once the child has prayed, read Hebrews 13:5b and 6a. Ask, *"What has Jesus done for you?"* This will give assurance of salvation.

Pray for that child when you are finished. Then have the child choose at least one person to tell about what happened (usually a parent).

Rejoice with the family!

It is possible you might have a situation that includes parents who are not happy about the choice made by their child. If this happens, explain the decision to the parents, but then, if at all possible, disciple that child yourself. If the child goes to another church or no church at all, check on the child when you can. Definitely pray for that young Christian.

Be sure to tell your pastor of the child's decision so he can follow up with the family and discuss baptism. If you are a parent and your child has accepted Jesus as his or her Savior, be sure to help your child grow in knowledge and service.

Consider giving the child a copy of **Mateo's Choice** to help disciple him and share the gospel with his family.

# HOW TO BECOME AN EXCELLENT BIBLE TEACHER

■ ■ ■ ■ ■ ■ ■ ■ ■ ■ ■ ■ ■ ■ ■ ■ ■ ■ ■ ■ ■ ■

When teaching children, our goal is two-fold. First, we want kids to **get right** with God through a saving faith. Second, we want our children to **stay right** with God through the sanctification process.

> You, however, continue in the things you have learned and become convinced of, knowing from whom you have learned them, and that from childhood you have known the sacred writings which are able to give you the wisdom that leads to salvation through faith which is in Christ Jesus. All Scripture is inspired by God and profitable for teaching, for reproof, for correction, for training in righteousness; so that the man of God may be adequate, equipped for every good work.
>
> 2 Timothy 3:14-17 (NASB)

**WHAT We Want to Teach:**

We want to focus on verse 16, because if we can (1) **teach** doctrine in a way that reveals sin, and then (2) explain how to stop sinning (**reproof**), and then (3) counsel children how to fix their sin problems (**correction**), THEN (4) they will be restored to a character of **righteousness** so God can use them for good works. This is the cycle of sanctification after salvation. All of this happens through the power of the Holy Spirit.

However, the cycle of sanctification does not revolve in a circle. It is more like a spiral as we grow closer to God and He works on our hearts.

We can also think of it this way: As our view of God increases, our view of ourselves decreases. (Sounds like John the Baptist!) The discrepancy is seen more and more. Jesus becomes bigger in our lives the more we know of Him. He must increase. We must decrease. Yes, we are children of God and heirs to a Kingdom, but we are clothed in unrighteous rags. We need Jesus.

This is what we want for our children, whether they are our own or those we teach in the church. **We want them to view Jesus as being the One and Only Greatest Person in their lives.**

## HOW We Teach This:

In order to be an excellent Bible teacher, a person must seek God first and foremost. **I fail at this.** I am not an excellent Bible teacher because of what I do, but because of what God chooses to do through me. I attempt to read the Bible every day. I attempt to make good choices. I mess up.

I think this is what makes the difference between a mediocre Bible teacher and an excellent Bible teacher: **An excellent Bible teacher daily recognizes his or her own need for a Savior**.

It is through our failings that Christ shines His light into our Bible lessons. When we explain to children how God is real, forgiving, and personal in our own lives, they will begin to search for that type of relationship as well.

**How do we teach children? By allowing God to teach us.** This means we need to take an honest look at ourselves, evaluate our hearts, and apply what God shows us to our teaching.

***Prayerfully read through the next few questions and answer them.***

*Evaluation of Yourself:*

1. Are you sold out to Jesus?
2. How enthusiastic are you about your teaching?
3. Are you interested in your children's lives?
4. Can you sense the needs of your children?
5. Are you a servant leader?

*Evaluation of Each Bible Lesson:*

1. Did you accomplish your objectives?
2. If not, why?
3. What was weak?

4. What was strong?

5. What changes should you make before the next lesson or before you teach this lesson again?

*Evaluation of the Teaching Year:*

1. How many salvations took place among your children?

2. Can you see a growth of Biblical knowledge in your children?

3. Was there growth in their spiritual heart knowledge?

> "To whom would He teach knowledge,
> And to whom would He interpret the message?
> Those just weaned from milk?
> Those just taken from the breast?
>
> "For He says,
> 'Order on order, order on order,
> Line on line, line on line,
> A little here, a little there.'"
>
> Isaiah 28:9-10 (NASB)

Biblical knowledge, or learning the Scriptures, takes a life time. It involves a little truth here and a little lesson there, step by step. We Bible teachers want our children to discover for themselves what they *ought* to do, so that through loving God, they will *obey* Him regardless of any obstacles. **A committed will to obey God equals a changed life.**

If you would like to have more training to improve your Bible Teaching skills, consider purchasing the 5 part video series course Becoming an Excellent Bible Teacher (https://futureflyingsaucers-bible-insitute.teachable.com/p/excellent-bible-teacher).

# A NOTE FROM THE AUTHOR

Friend, I encourage you. You hold the living, powerful Word of God in your hands. Use it wisely. Read it lovingly. Teach from it enthusiastically. Love powerfully. **Be Excellent!**

Your Servant,

Anne Marie
FutureFlyingSaucers.com

# COLORING PAGES

Today a Savior,
who is Messiah the Lord,
was born for you
in the city of David.

—Luke 2: 11 (HCSB)

Jesus continued to learn more
and more and to grow physically.
People liked him, and he pleased God.

—Luke 2:52 (ICB)

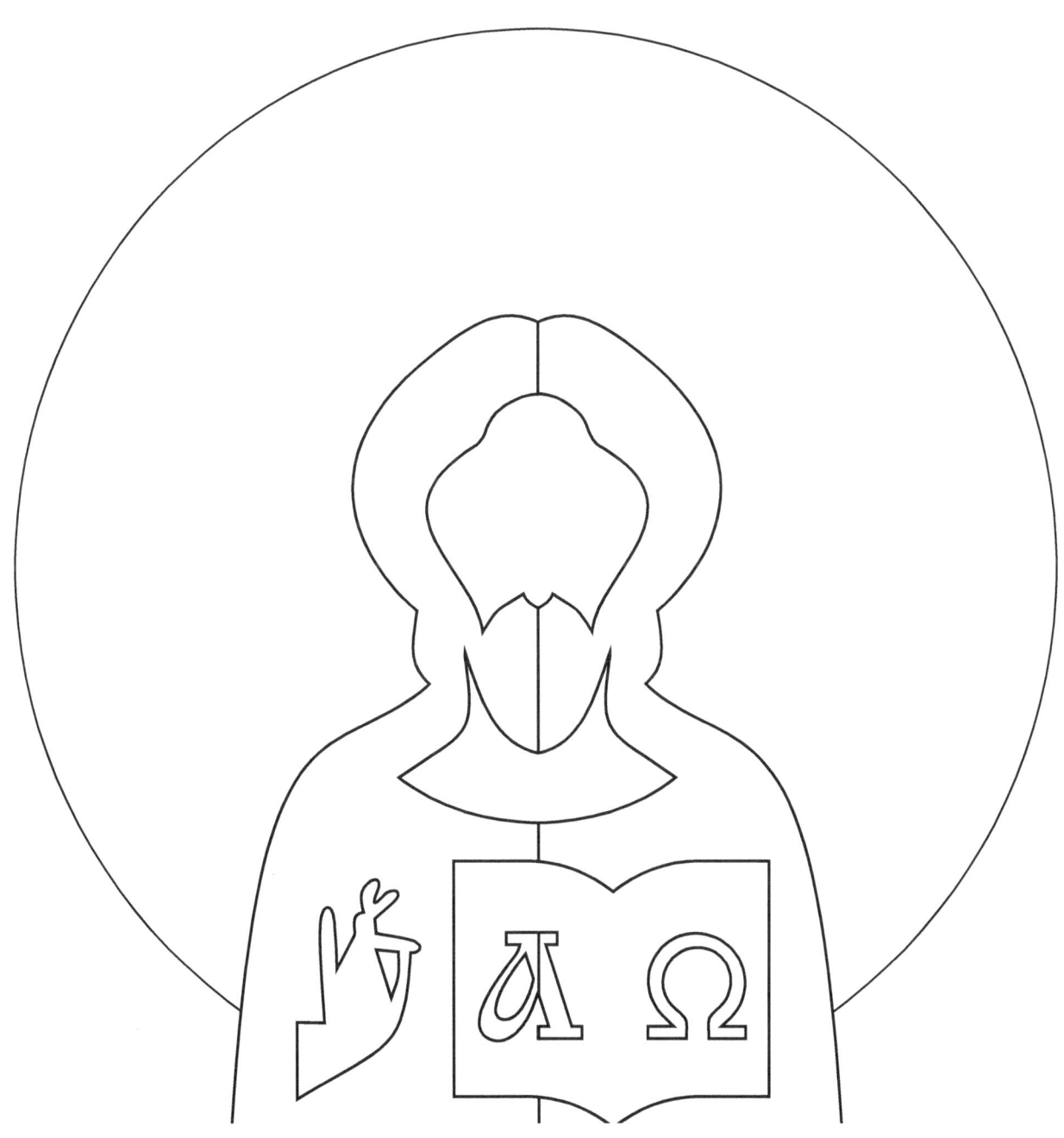

FUTUREFLYINGSAUCERS.COM

John answered everyone,

"I baptize you with water, but there is one coming later who can do more than I can. I am not good enough to untie his sandals. He will baptize you with the Holy Spirit and with fire."

—Luke 3:16 (ICB)

Then Jesus returned from the Jordan, full of the **Holy Spirit,** and was led by the Spirit in the wilderness.

—Luke 4:1 (HCSB)

futureflyingsaucers.com

Jesus said to them,

Come and follow me.
I will make you
fishermen for men.

—Mark 1:17 (ICB)

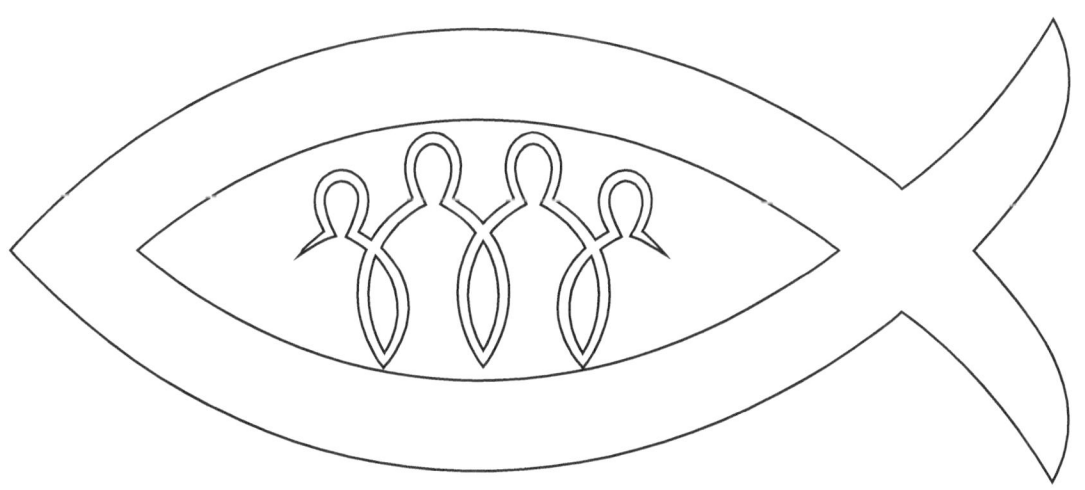

For GOD so loved THE WORLD that he GAVE his one & only Son, THAT WHOEVER BELIEVES IN HIM SHALL NOT PERISH BUT HAVE Eternal life
JOHN 3:16
(NIV)

# Immediately

the man was well. He picked up his mat and started walking. The day all this happened was a Sabbath day.

—John 5:9 (ESV)

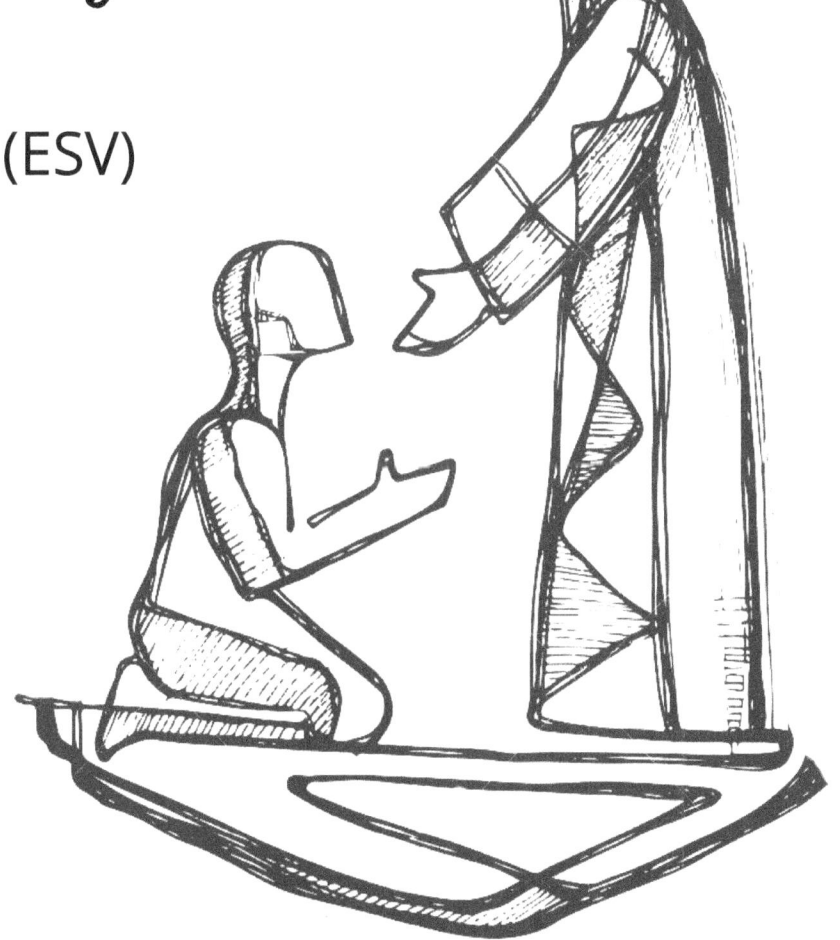

Everyone who sees the Son and believes in him has eternal life. I will raise him up on the last day. This is what my Father wants.

—John 6:40 (ICB)

Those people who know they have great spiritual needs are

# HAPPY.

The kingdom of heaven belongs to them.

—Matthew 5:3 (ICB)

As long as I am in the WORLD, I AM the LIGHT of the world.

—John 9:5 (HCSB)

The kingdom of heaven is like
# TREASURE,
buried in a field, that a man found and reburied. Then in his joy he goes and sells everything he has and buys that field.

—Matthew 13:44 (HCSB)

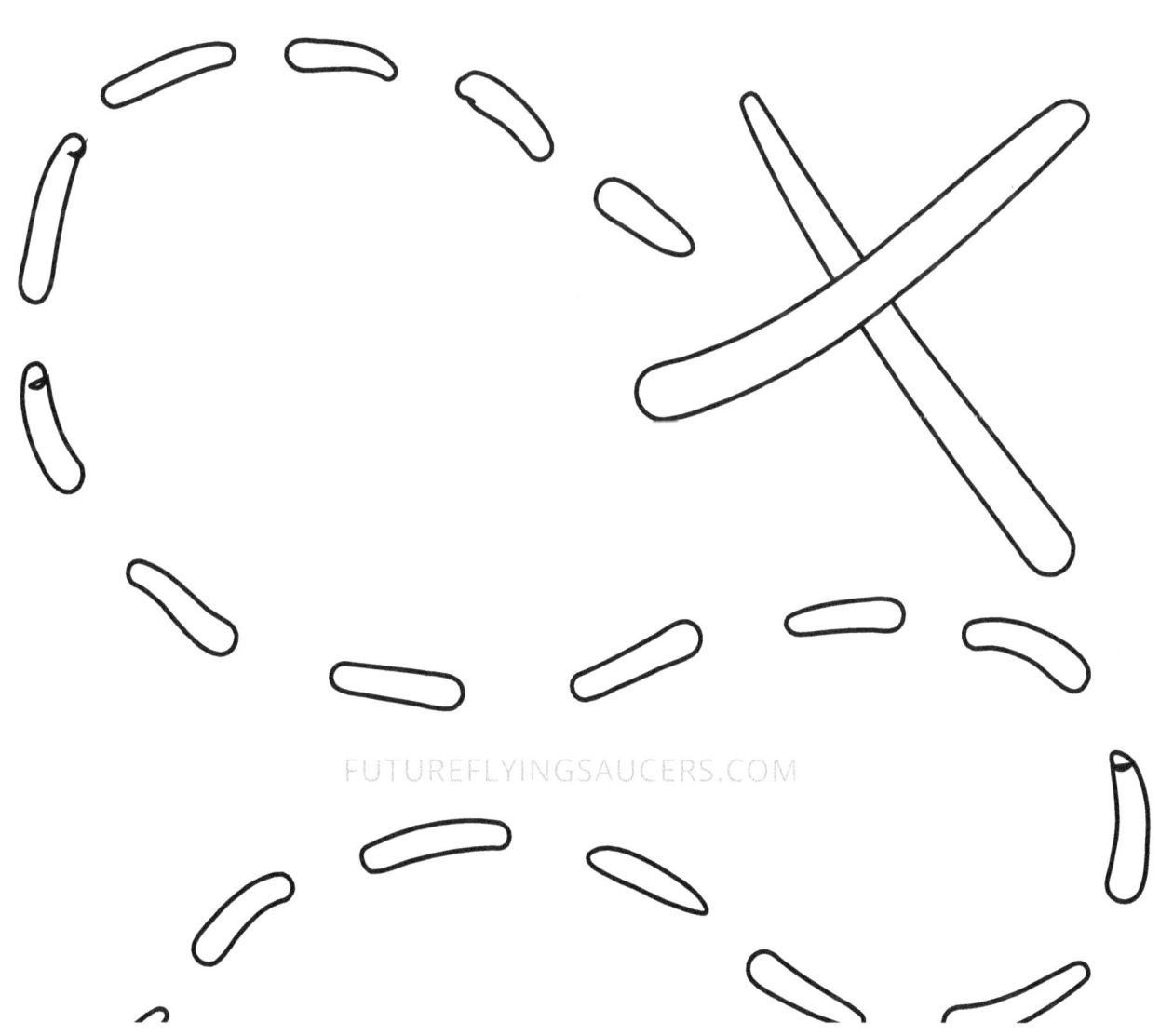

FUTUREFLYINGSAUCERS.COM

# I am the door.

The person who enters through me WILL BE SAVED. He will be able to COME IN and go out and find pasture.

—John 10:9 (ICB)

"I did this as an example for you. So you should do as I have done for you.

—John 13:15 (ICB)

# Then Jesus cried in a loud voice and died.

—Mark 15:37 (ICB)

But he is not here.
He has risen from death
as he said he would.
Come and see the place
where his body was.

—Matthew 28:6 (ICB)

They said to each other,
"When Jesus talked to us on the road,
it felt like a fire burning in us.
It was exciting when he explained
the true meaning of the Scriptures."

—Luke 24:32 (ICB)

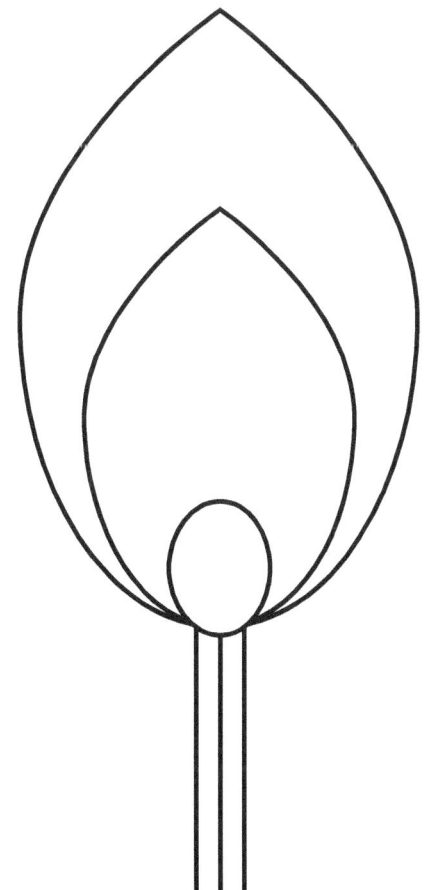

Jesus said to them,

"Come and eat."

None of the followers dared ask him,

"Who are you?"

They knew it was the Lord.

—John 21:12 (ICB)

But the HOLY SPIRIT will come to you.
Then you will receive POWER.
YOU WILL BE my witnesses—
in Jerusalem, in all of Judea, in Samaria,
and in EVERY PART of the world.

—Acts 1:8 (ICB)